SINÉAD

Andrew Macpherson

SINÉAD

Her Life and Music

Jimmy Guterman

WARNER BOOKS

A Time Warner Company

Warner Books, Inc., 666 Fifth Avenue, New York, NY 10103
A Time Warner Company

Printed in the United States of America
First printing: February 1991
10 9 8 7 6 5 4 3 2 1

Library of Congress Cataloging-in-Publication Data

Guterman, Jimmy.
   Sinead / Jimmy Guterman.
      p.   cm.
   Summary: Portrays the life and music of the Irish singer who has
been called the first major pop star of the 1990s.
   ISBN 0-446-39254-5
   1. O'Connor, Sinead.   2. Rock musicians—Ireland—Biography.
[1. O'Connor, Sinead.   2. Singers.   3. Rock music.]   I. Title.
ML420.0297G9 1991
782.42166'092—dc20
[B]
[92]
                                    90-46825
                                         CIP
                                    AC MN

Book design by Giorgetta Bell McRee

Cover photograph by Christine Alicino

Cover design by John Beng

For Jane Kokernak

AUTHOR'S NOTE

I do not know what grade Sinéad O'Connor got in math class when she was eleven years old; I do not care whether she breast-fed her son. These sorts of intrusive factoids, masquerading as revelations, that add up to biographies of pop stars are in fact none of our business.

More important, such information is usually not helpful toward understanding someone's music or its context. Journalists should not be afraid (or too lazy) to pay more attention to Sinéad's work and waste less ink on her hair length and marital status.

What is interesting about Sinéad, more than the private specifics of her life, is her music and its ramifications. Sinéad is only twenty-four and has put out only two albums but her music and conduct have raised more provocative issues than most rock-and-roll performers do in their entire careers. How does someone become a superstar with intentionally insular music? How do folk-tinged ballads top the charts in these dance-heavy times? How does a bald woman become a sex symbol? These are issues worth exploring; these are the issues that are more interesting than whether Sinéad cuts her own hair or what really went on between her and her opening act, singer Hugh Harris.

Yet Sinéad herself makes it difficult to approach the music in isolation. Even if her songs are not literal autobiography (a songwriter cannot use true-life experiences without altering them), she does present them as at least metaphorical autobiography, so it is impossible to dive into her music without bumping into the artist.

When Sinéad tells an interviewer, "All the songs are autobiographical," and then adds, "Whatever I have to discuss is discussed in the songs," she insists we make some conjectures about her when we hear her music; if we do so without making ridiculous leaps, we can arrive at a deeper appreciation of the songs and the woman who sings them. It might even make listening to her records more fun.

Jimmy Guterman
October 1990

I refer to Sinéad throughout the book by her first name, because that is the way she identifies herself. Her music is about familiarity; using her last name would create distance.

SINÉAD

1

The Navy Blue Bird

Sinéad O'Connor is precisely what she claims she does not want to be: she is a famous pop star. Whether she is singing one of her hits before a sold-out auditorium or delineating one of her controversial views for a spellbound reporter, she is working in one place: the arena of public view. She may say she does not like it, but she is living an extremely public life.

When she is onstage, Sinéad comes as close as she can to being before people and still managing to control her environment. And on the tour behind her multiplatinum second album, **I Do Not Want What I Haven't Got**, she has an audience primed to respond to her slightest move. She has an audience anxious for such control. When the house lights go down, Sinéad is greeted by a roar far different from the Pavlovian one that, say, heavy metal bands have gotten used to when their roadies switch on their battery of dry-ice fog machines. Characterizing a roar is a treacherous undertaking, but anyone who has been to more than a few rock concerts can tell the difference between a mere awakening roar and a truly anticipatory one. Listen to the intensity: this is undoubtedly the latter. Sinéad's legions are attracted to her, by and large, because they sense that she is a real person writing and singing about emotional experiences with which they can identify. Of course they are going to roar: the dimming of the lights reminds them of the connection they feel with Sinéad, and they are bracing for a powerful introduction.

They get one. The stage still black, the thirteen-song set begins with her taped voice intoning the spoken section that launches "Feel So Different," the first cut on **I Do Not Want What I Haven't Got**. The crowd's roar explodes from anticipation into recognition as it hears, "God, grant me the serenity to accept the things I cannot change, the courage to change the things I can, and the wisdom to know the difference." Synthesizers swirl behind her words. Sinéad is reciting a prayer familiar to anyone who ever wandered into one of the many Twelve Step recovery groups that proliferated in the 1980s, so there is now recognition on several levels.

Two spotlights flash to life and converge on her at center stage. Wearing a tight floral-print outfit that looks like a modified one-piece bathing suit ending in shorts (this is one of the few get-ups she wears onstage lately that does not hang loose), she pivots against the microphone stand and burrows into the song. The brightness of the lights accentuates her slimness as well as her baldness. Cushioned by synthesizers that grow more stately as the song progresses, "Feel So Different" is a statement of purpose, both for Sinéad and her audience.

For those who did not care much for her debut LP **The Lion and the Cobra** (and there must be many of them in the crowd; it has sold barely one-fifth as many copies as its follow-up), both on record and in concert "Feel So Differ-

4

ent" kicks off a listening experience by announcing that something new is happening with Sinéad and her work. "I am not like I was before," she sings slowly and intently, and it is no empty rock-star boast. She sounds in control but searching; in short, she sounds like an artist.

Yet it is the icon Sinéad getting as much notice as the artist Sinéad tonight. Her slightest hand gesture or increase in vocal volume elicits automatic screams; all she needs to do to earn cheers that nearly drown her out is move one of her black boots an inch or underline the synthesizer lines of keyboardists Mark Taylor and Susan Davis with a mild wiggle of her hips. She is singing an intensely personal song—a quiet one, with no drums or percussion to draw out the tale into the light—yet the volume and intensity of her audience is more along the lines of what one would expect at a New Kids on the Block lip-synching event. Sinéad's fans often assert that they are attracted to her because they find her a challenging low-tech alternative to video-contrived dance acts like Milli Vanilli and Paula Abdul, but right now these fans are cheering an image. Screaming so loudly, they cannot hear the music—there is nothing that they can be responding to except Sinéad's image, even if it is an anti-image.

"Feel So Different" ascends to a climax, and, after quickly securing a twelve-string acoustic guitar, Sinéad rocks out and the audience returns to its feet. She guides her five-piece band (the two keyboardists plus guitarist Marco Pirroni, bassist Dean Garcia, and drummer David Ruffy) through a hard version of "The Emperor's New Clothes," a broad, sturdy rocker from the recent album that serves as both a love note and put-down. Sinéad bounces across the stage as a slide of her face appears on an enormous rear-projection screen; again the low-key honesty of the song is countered by an intrusive icon.

Veteran guitarist Pirroni offers up some chunky lead lines that should be looser, but Sinéad sings rough, sings like a punk. She pushes across the vulnerable lines and the defiant lines of the impressionistic tale with the same tenacity. She stares straight ahead, strums her guitar, and sings loud. Whether it is a synthesizer ballad without drums like "Feel So Different" or an electric rocker like "The Emperor's New Clothes" that she is performing, Sinéad is just as intent. There's joy in the crowd, but it is hard to find any onstage.

Then Sinéad breaks the tension and tries to loosen up both herself and her audience. She sets aside her guitar and careers into "I Want Your (Hands on Me)," one of the few songs from the first album strong enough to survive when played after a track from the second. "I Want Your (Hands on Me)" is meant as a funk workout, but although Sinéad twitches her hands and body as she emotes the song's declaration of tough and unbridled lust, she is not naturally funky. It is no accident that when Sinéad first attempted to remix this cut for dance clubs, she enlisted the help of genuine rapper M. C. Lyte. Sinéad rubs her hands up and down her torso, teasing in the manner crowds have comes to expect of performers like Prince and Madonna (who in part also got the idea from the Minneapolis dervish).

But Sinéad is not trying to replicate the moves of a dancer like Cat Glover (from Prince's **Sign o' the Times**—era outfit) and her turbulent moves are too spontaneous for her to have to suffer the "thinking man's Madonna" tag that superficial rock critics have hung on her. Unlike the work of Prince or Madonna, artifice is only a small part of the sexual cry of Sinéad's "I Want Your (Hands on Me)." Her moves are unstudied and for the most part unchoreographed; Sinéad is acting out the song and not milking it. The crowd moves with her.

This is but one stop of the ninety-minute trip through which Sinéad leads her audience. Also, unlike Prince or Madonna (or the majority of the day's music-video icons), she doesn't present her live show as part of a progressive striptease—unless one wants to consider this show an emotional striptease in which Sinéad gradually tells more personal stories.

The next two songs—"Three Babies" and "Black Boys on Mopeds"—are among the quietest entries on **I Do Not Want What I Haven't Got** and they reveal someone with far more on her mind than the next coupling (Prince and Madonna have wide world views, too, but they almost always wind up focusing on sex and power). "Three Babies," on which she and her twelve-string acoustic are augmented only by two keyboards, is a devotional tune, verging on being specifically religious, that at once shows off the range of her voice and the range of her concerns as a songwriter. Yet "Three Babies," which elliptically celebrates hard-fought monogamy and motherhood, must be a tough performance for her to include in every show nowadays. Her three-year-old son, Jake, is an ocean away in England; her second separation from her husband (and former drummer), John Reynolds, has been well documented; and her brief affair with singer Hugh Harris opened old wounds and caused a few new ones. It is a tribute to the commitment of the song—and Sinéad's commitment to it—that not a moment sounds false. By the end of the last verse, Sinéad is short of breath; but the moment she stops singing, fans shout. Keyboards swell, the adoring crowd cheers, and Sinéad's quick smile before she turns away from the audience suggests that she is a bit embarrassed by such adulation.

"Black Boys on Mopeds" reminds the crowd that even on her quietest songs, Sinéad can be ferocious. It is the most bitter number on **I Do Not Want What I Haven't Got** (quite an achievement, when you consider such songs as "The Last Day of Our Acquaintance" and "You Cause as Much Sorrow") as well as the most complex. Full of purposeful hyperbole and exaggeration that suggest thoughtful experience rather than the received dogma that sometimes shaped **The Lion and the Cobra**, "Black Boys on Mopeds" centers on the senseless murder of a young man and expands the story to damn the shambles that is Margaret Thatcher's England. The arrangement is stripped down, just Sinéad on guitar and keyboardist Davis adding a second acoustic guitar and harmonies. The crowd is at odds with this quiet, deliberate sound. The noise is far different from the usual arena-rock-crowd restlessness during slow songs, but it does threaten to overtake the intent singer. Yet those listening closely can pick up two lines that hint at the core of her music.

Sinéad sets the scene of a young mother out in the cold at five in the morning foraging for food in piles of the previous night's restaurant garbage, and adds "in her arms she holds three cold babies." It is a vivid, compact line that directly refers to both the "Three Babies" of the song she just sang and (even if Sinéad is not aware of it) Dorothea Lange's 1936 photograph of a Depression-ravaged "Migrant Mother" in Nipomo, California, trying to find enough strength to care for her three hungry, dirty children. But for Sinéad this is not a there-but-for-the-grace-of-God-go-I reference that makes us care more for the singer than the subject; it is a straightforward description all the more chilling for its simplicity.

In the chorus, Sinéad reveals her musical soul when she sings, "England's not the mythical land of Madame George and roses." It is a line intended to demythologize Merry

Olde England, but it also shows how deeply Sinéad has bought into another set of myths: those written by fellow Irish soul singer and mystic Van Morrison. A song called "Madame George" is the centerpiece of Morrison's 1968 album **Astral Weeks**; it is the cornerstone of Morrison's reputation as the only performer who can summon up and then outmatch Ray Charles and William Butler Yeats in a single vocal or lyrical outburst. Sinéad's music is as rootless and original as anyone's in pop music today, but she had to come from somewhere, and the possibilities raised by Van Morrison's uncompromising song cycles are without a doubt that somewhere. "Black Boys on Mopeds" culminates in a wordless moan that segues into fan screams.

These are personal songs Sinéad is singing tonight; even if they are not as autobiographical as some of her fans and critics like to assert in attempts to appear close to the performer whose work is more intimate than some friendships; they sound like song-stories that should be told in a coffeehouse or a living room, not in a sold-out arena with eight thousand of the faithful serving rowdy, sing-along witness. Sinéad is spared the audible distraction during her songs—instead of floor-hogging monitors, she hears herself and her band through earphones—but between songs she mostly smiles and looks uncomfortable as an object of fan worship. "I'm the most boring person in the world," she says softly after she finishes "Black Boys on Mopeds." "So all I can say is thank you very much." The adoration increases several more decibels.

Alone in the center of the large stage, Sinéad presents "Jackie," the first song on her first record. The performance tonight is stark but the song itself is no more than adequate; more than anything else it underlines how much Sinéad grew as a writer between her first and second albums. Couplets like "Jackie's gone/She's lost in the rain" make it sound like she is searching for a truant cocker spaniel. Nearly a million people bought **The Lion and the Cobra** so there is no way that Sinéad will not play selections from it, but with the exception of "I Want Your (Hands on Me)" and "Mandinka" (the guitar cruncher with which she closes her sets) none of the numbers from the earlier disk survive scrutiny when compared to her more recent, more personal, more trustworthy songs. Yet Sinéad the performer surpasses Sinéad the songwriter tonight; at the very least the audience presumes that she believes what she is singing. Since performance of rock songs is more important than composition, Sinéad holds sway.

"Jackie" ends quickly enough and what follows imme-diately erases its shortcomings from memory. A roadie places a reel-to-reel tape player next to Sinéad, who is still alone onstage, and she switches it on. The show peaks on "I Am Stretched on Your Grave," the macabre Frank O'Connor poem that Sinéad O'Connor married to a drum rhythm sampled from James Brown's much-pillaged 1970 hit "Funky Drummer." The poem is classic Irish Gothic— the narrator lives what appears to be a normal life but in fact spends nights prostrate upon the final resting place of a childhood sweetheart—and such sentiments are a natural for a connoisseur of the Romantic like Sinéad. As disconcerting as it may seem at first, the combination of the Irish poem and the African-American beat is seamless. The work of James Brown drummer Clyde Stubblefield, as stalwart fans of the Godfather of Soul know, is malleable enough to include damn near everything anyone can throw at it. For the first time in the show, the crowd is not just standing up and swaying; the audience is dancing.

The instrumental coda of "I Am Stretched on Your

Grave," augmented by a taped fiddle, is a long one (a characteristic of many of the songs on **I Do Not Want What I Haven't Got**), and it is one in which Sinéad clearly wants to join her fans and not merely sway but truly **move**. She is not much of a dancer, as "I Want Your (Hands on Me)" testified minutes ago, but she is so transported by the beat of "I Am Stretched on Your Grave" that she will do anything to become part of it. Sinéad offers a sort of reconstructed jig with military-march overtones; she may not be Paula Abdul, but there is no way she is going to sit on a folkie's stool and strum an acoustic guitar while Stubblefield's inarguable beat fills the night air.

Sinéad's music grew out of the American and British folk traditions—her earliest gigs featured her warbling comeback-period Bob Dylan tunes in Dublin coffeehouses—but such traditions are simply touchstones, not roots to which she remains stubbornly entangled. Folk music is a sound for Sinéad, an arbitrary starting point. These days what she listens to most frequently and readily is the hard-core rap of Public Enemy and N.W.A. (Niggas with Attitude; Sinéad sometimes wears a P.W.A. T-shirt: Paddy with Attitude). In her reworking of the Frank O'Connor poem, Sinéad O'Connor unites the ostensibly disparate worlds of insular, poetic folk music and hard-core, beat-obsessed rap.

Such a fusion is the unequivocal high point of the evening, but that does not mean that anyone who leaves early is not going to miss something wonderful. The remaining performances are insouciant and trenchant enough to keep the crowd members chewing them over for days to come. And as a plus, all the instruments are being played live, a practice that is becoming an anomaly in arena shows. These songs are more lively than any backing-tape set will ever be. "The Last Day of Our Acquaintance" is at once both vulnerable and disobedient; "Jump in the River" is a dissonant scorcher; "Mandinka" is an even tauter rocker on which Pirroni's guitar finally blazes through; and "Troy," which Sinéad performs alone with her twelve-string acoustic guitar to end the concert, is a bitter benediction that hushes the crowd.

Such silence is rare. The loudest roar of the night is reserved for the opening chords of "Nothing Compares 2 U," the Prince throwaway that Sinéad reimagined into a number one smash in eighteen countries. In the age of the power ballad—when hard-rock groups like Poison and Skid Row have more hit snoozers than middle-of-the-road crooners Kenny Rogers or Lionel Ritchie—Sinéad's "Nothing Compares 2 U" is a bracing restatement of a relative rarity nowadays, the great straight-ahead rock-and-roll ballad that is neither Tin Pan Alley slop nor a slowed-down heavy-metal groaner. Sinéad extends the unrequited love song in its live incarnation; although her five-piece band remains subdued throughout, Sinéad's vocal fireworks aim for the guitar pyrotechnics in rock's hopeless-love landmark, Derek and the Dominoes' "Layla." She is a professional throughout—every sly nuance in her vocal is well thought-out—yet the abandon with which she takes on "Nothing Compares 2 U" is not that of a professional working from her usual array of manipulative effects. Like Eric Clapton and Duane Allman on "Layla," Sinéad feels "Nothing Compares 2 U" more than she consciously understands it; it is that smart closeness to the material that makes it a ballad to which millions have immediately responded.

That immediacy is the essential facet of Sinéad's appeal. Those who respond to her rarely do so after prolonged exposure to her work: either they love it or they walk away. That nearly instantaneous performer-fan connection is virtually impossible in these days of radio narrowcasting and music-video barragement, in which the audience is instructed not only what music to hear, but is also given visual cues on how to interpret what they hear.

Sinéad's second album was a smash "out of the box." *I Do Not Want What I Haven't Got* was number one for six weeks and it leapfrogged to the top of the **Billboard** LP chart in only three weeks; "Nothing Compares 2 U," which stayed on top for a month, reached its top spot in only four weeks. Such alacrity is only expected of superstars who already have a massive audience. But many heard the record or saw the "Nothing Compares 2 U" video just once and joined up without asking questions. That is not supposed to happen in an industry that prides itself on steady, careful control of the fortunes of its performers. By comparison, the performer who succeeded Sinéad at the top of the charts triumphed in the more accepted way, by means of clever marketing, saturation airplay, and a just-familiar-enough tune. The success of M. C. Hammer's **Please Hammer Don't Hurt 'Em** album and "U Can't Touch This" single (a rap over the rhythm track of Rick James's 1981 hit "Super Freak") was long and hard-fought. Even with all the pieces in perfect order, **Please Hammer Don't Hurt 'Em** didn't hit the top spot until its fourth month of release. This is the way the music industry is supposed to work, as far as the executives, the programmers, and the promotion folks are concerned.

But Sinéad is different. Because she has earned the immediate loyalty of a market too large for record companies to dismiss, she can get away with gestures that even artists who sell more records cannot. As contradictory as it might seem, she uses this leverage as a means to focus the spotlight closer to her work, not her face. Fans who attend rock concerts spend not only twenty-odd dollars for a ticket, but they also buy official-artist merchandise like T-shirts and programs.

Sinéad offers such stuff, but with a difference. None of the many designs of T-shirts and sweat shirts bear her image; many of them do not even feature her name. In the title track of **I Do Not Want What I Haven't Got** she sings, ''I saw a navy blue bird/Flying way above the sea/I walked on and I learned later/That this navy blue bird was me,'' so many of the T-shirts have a navy blue bird on them. The T-shirts are secret membership cards; only fellow fans will understand what the bird means.

Sinéad survives callous jokes about the shortness of her hair and snide jingoistic comments on her quite public behavior. In interviews, she reveals only the information she deems necessary and is quick to cut off something she does not like. This can go to extremes. Sinéad used to tape interviews herself so she could challenge expected mis-quotes, and during her television interview with American newsbabe Maria Shriver she ordered a cameraman to stop filming her boots. (This order made it into the aired broadcast.) Sinéad wants to be a pop star, all right, but she insisted on becoming one and insists on remaining one on her own terms.

2

Ireland

*T*o hear Sinéad tell it, she has always been this way: headstrong, defiant, unwilling or unable to conform. She was born in the working-class Glenageary part of Dublin on December 8, 1966, and she was doomed to grow up unhappy in an Ireland (and as part of what she perceived as an oppressive, sexist faith) that did not allow divorce. Sinéad, the third of John and Marie O'Connor's four children, grew up cautiously, anxiously observing what was left of a marriage that had begun to deteriorate before she had been born.

John O'Connor was an engineer (he later took up law) and Marie was a dressmaker before they wed. They had married young, too young they both admitted in retrospect, and Sinéad and her two brothers and one sister spent their early years in a home full of constant strife, all anger and precarious silences. From all reports, Marie felt suffocated by the relationship. She felt the responsibilities of marriage and the children deprived her of a real professional career, but Marie and John's adherence to Catholicism's insistence on a permanent marriage, no matter what, led to an uneasy existence that sometimes accelerated into violence. (Sinéad's interview comments frequently refer to a childhood speckled by unspecified "abuse.") In 1975, John and Marie finally separated (as Irish Catholics, they could not divorce) and for the next five years Sinéad lived with her mother almost all the time.

When she was thirteen, Sinéad started doing what most thirteen-year-old kids, from happy homes or not, start doing: she rebelled. Sinéad has said that her five years in the home of her mother were dark and for the most part joyless, and at thirteen she moved back in with her father. Sinéad saw little of her mother over the next few years; when Marie O'Connor was killed in a car crash in 1985, she had not seen her daughter in more than a year. It is neither a stretch nor obtrusive to suggest that the lack of resolution in such an important life relationship informs Sinéad's work, and the artist herself has acknowledged as much. **The Lion and the Cobra** is dedicated to Marie O'Connor; perhaps to keep balance, Sinéad dedicated **I Do Not Want What I Haven't Got** to her father, although in significantly warmer terms.

By all accounts, John O'Connor seems to have kept his daughter on a longer leash than his wife did. Again, Sinéad responded like a typical adolescent by seeing how far she could tug without being yanked back. She skipped school regularly enough to be considered a truant by school officials, and she spent much of her hooky time moping around Dublin and playing video games. She funded her Space Invaders habit by pilfering cash out of her father's wallet. Having gotten away with that minor offense, she moved on to shoplifting clothes and perfume, and eventually got caught trying to sneak out of a store with a pair of unpaid-for shoes. Sinéad's violations of the law were extremely minor compared to much of the ugliness with which a young teenager can find herself involved. Sinéad, her interviewers, and her fans are fond of romanticizing her upbringing into one that recalls Charles Dickens's **Hard Times**, but such mythmaking on the part of others suggests that none of them remember what it was like being thirteen.

Still, these infractions worried John O'Connor enough that he decided he had to place his daughter in a situation that might teach her some discipline. Sinéad breezed from strict school to strict school, among them the boarding school Mayfield College in Drumcondra, until she settled in at the Newton School in Waterford, several hours' drive south of Dublin.

Sinéad has insisted that those were difficult years of internment for her (she still speaks with derision of the Dominican nuns who watched over her soul at Blackrock's Sion Hill School), but it was also the time period during which she realized what she wanted to do with her life. She played guitar in her dormitory room, began to feel comfortable singing and even writing the beginnings of songs (some of which she still performs), and found some solace through her music. The development was slow but aided by the lack of distractions; this was, after all, convent life.

Not surprisingly, this period of Sinéad's life was also fraught with tremendous ambivalence about organized religion. As she told **Q**'s Mark Cooper, "When you grow up in Ireland, you aspire to being like the Virgin Mary. Irish women are brought up to look up to the Mother of God and have this obsession with purity and chastity." The combination of wanting to break out artistically and at the same time being repressed emotionally (or feeling that she was being repressed emotionally) by the nuns caring for her left Sinéad in some ways more confused than she was when she got to the respective institutions. But she also got support for her nascent talents from some of her teachers, and she has never completely walked away from her religious upbringing. No one has acknowledged the religious and spiritual qualities of her work more than she; as much as she damns organized religion, it is frequently on her mind. She told **SPIN** that as a child she was obsessed with St. Bernadette and wanted to become a nun.

Sinéad's first break came when one of her teachers at Mayfield asked Sinéad to sing at her wedding. Sinéad warbled a version of "Evergreen," the Barbra Streisand hit from **A Star Is Born**, a film allegedly about rock and roll. (Sinéad was a big fan of Streisand's musicals.) Sinéad's performance of the tune would have been just another step in her development—first time singing before lots of people and all that—except that the brother of the bride was Paul Byrne, drummer for the band In Tua Nua.

Byrne and Sinéad became fast friends and Sinéad wound up helping write the group's first single, "Take My Hand." More than six years later, the rare track (Sinéad's subsequent superstardom has made the Island Records 45-rpm disc something of a collector's item) sounds like a wan composition with promise, one worthy of precisely the minimal notice it received. "Take My Hand" is pleasant enough folkish rock, but it does not offer any of the energy or—more important—any of the experience of Sinéad's subsequent work. The most positive spin to put on it is to respond to it as the sound of a young talent starting to find her way; not bad for a fifteen-year-old kid who a year earlier had no direction.

Early tracks often are the surest clues to revealing a performer's musical roots, but those looking to "Take My

Hand" for such information will be disappointed. Its folk-rock is generic enough to have sprung from sources as diverse as Richard Thompson's ominous staggers or Joni Mitchell's more elliptical pronouncements, which is as broad as that territory runs. Sinéad and In Tua Nua are only two of the Irish rock performers for whom such where-did-their-ideas-come-from detective work is fruitless. Someone of Sinéad's talent cannot help but be a true original. (Back to the **SPIN** article, the interviewer claims to have played her Patti Smith's "Piss Factory" and Richard Hell's "Blank Generation," neither of which she cared for, and the New York Dolls, whom she had never heard of. So much for her alleged roots in the New York punk scene.)

The lack of clear influences in In Tua Nua leads to the fundamental fact of Irish rock and roll, which is its brazen — and necessary—rootlessness. Rootlessness is an essential element in every country's rock-and-roll scene except that of the United States, where rootlessness is a synonym for opportunism or laziness. Rock and roll was born out of all American forms, notably country and western, rural and urban blues, and black gospel. (All rock-influencing forms are eventually traceable to Africa, but rock and roll from 1954 on is more directly based upon its American antecedents.)

There are periodic British invasions of American airwaves, in which new sounds—which the British bands invariably fashion out of predominantly American sources—are fed back to American ears. In the early 1980s, the most appealing and one of the most successful British bands taking over the charts in the United States was Culture Club, a quartet that enlivened a host of 1960s American rock and soul forms, particularly those of Motown Records. The American audience responded to the music, all right; but we also were enamored by the fact that the lead singer, Boy George, was a six-foot-tall, dreadlocked transvestite who could out-dish Joan Rivers. All British bands (and by extension all bands from outside the United States), whether they know it or not, are using musical tools invented in the American South. If a performer claims that his or her roots are in the seminal British bands the Beatles and the Rolling Stones, chances are that he or she is really rooted in something that has been filtered through the Beatles and the Rolling Stones.

The most obvious example of this rootlessness is that of the most popular of all Irish rock bands, U2, a group with both visionary and bombastic tendencies that would for a time serve as an important sponsor for Sinéad. There was much talk around the time U2's **Rattle and Hum** collection (the follow-up to its record-breaking **The Joshua Tree**) came out that the record and the film of the same title were about the group's "search for its roots." (Much of this talk came from the advertising and promotional material for the film, so it was what the band members wanted its audience to think.) **Rattle and Hum** was the quartet's sixth album (eighth if you count live EPs); it seemed absurd that after more than eight years together the group would finally be getting around to discovering its roots.

Rather, what Irish bands like U2 excel in is deciding which outside roots to claim for itself. Since there are no genuine Irish rock-and-roll roots (sole exception: Van Morrison's Them, which made unique, doomy Irish blues-rock in much the same way the early Rolling Stones manufactured a similar British mélange), Irish rock bands have to go overseas to find a tradition that suits them. U2 started in 1980 with **Boy**, a terrific debut that expanded on sources as diverse as Led Zeppelin and the Sex Pistols, each in its own way a quintessential British rock-and-roll band that scattered American forms. U2 subsequently felt their way through a variety of styles, some of them exhilarating (the precise, hard-thinking rock of 1983's **War**), some of them disconcerting (the hazy art-rock posturings of **The Unforgettable Fire**, released the following year). When U2 singer Bono (né: Paul Hewson) sang a tune called, "I Still Haven't Found What I'm Looking For," he was addressing more than only spiritual concerns.

But **Rattle and Hum** found U2, like many non-American rock bands before them, searching for their "roots" an ocean away from home, in the United States. They recorded several tracks at Sun Studio in Memphis, Tennessee, the original home of Howlin' Wolf, Roy Orbison, Charlie Rich, Roscoe Gordon, and the Million Dollar Quartet: Elvis Presley, Jerry Lee Lewis, Carl Perkins, and Johnny Cash. At Sun, U2 were accompanied by the horn section behind the many marvelous Stax soul hits of the sixties and early seventies. Among U2's Sun tracks were a duet with blues giant B. B. King and a tribute to singer Billie Holiday over chord changes swiped from "Like a Rolling Stone" by Bob Dylan (Dylan pops up throughout the double record as a cherished, albeit desiccated, touchstone). U2 aspired for the "honesty" they sensed in their perceived antecedents, and they figured that recording in the same places as some of those people would yield similar results.

Not only are these sources—Sun, Stax, Dylan, American electric-urban blues—miles away from the grand sound U2 usually makes, but they are almost as far away from U2's original heroes. U2 are fans of these various purveyors of American music, and sometimes they are intelligent and respectful enough fans to operate well in those adopted forms. But U2's decision to become more of an "American music" band was a conscious, intellectual one, not a natural reaction to what they had heard in their home environment. They were attracted to these disparate forms after the better part of a decade on the road; they became popularizers. Rock-and-roll bands spend much—maybe too much—of their time traveling from city to city. It is no surprise, then, that for many bands (especially Irish ones, who have to go overseas if they intend to tour for more than a week) this physical rootlessness is preceded and mirrored by musical rootlessness.

This rootlessness is also true of the other Irish bands that have made noise in recent years. Ireland's major punk bands (Stiff Little Fingers, That Petrol Emotion) have nothing distinctly Irish branded on their work, and even bands more worthy (like Thin Lizzy) and less worthy (like the Boomtown Rats) looked to Great Britain and eventually the United States for cues. The Pogues acknowledge pre-rock Irish music by revving it up into a joke; Clannad, Steeleye Span, and the Chieftains sidestep the issue by avoiding pop music altogether and digging into tradition.

What a great Irish artist can pull off is exemplified by the career of Van Morrison, the performer who is Sinéad's clearest—and perhaps only—Irish antecedent. In the mid-sixties Morrison led the Belfast-based group Them, a blues-oriented outfit as devoted as the early Rolling Stones and, on record at least, even more ferocious. Their signature tune, "Gloria," has become a deserved rock standard, and such music is the standard against which all other Irish bands must be measured.

When Them broke up, Morrison moved to the United States and recorded a series of magnificent records that fused Celtic soul (musical and otherwise) with American pop. He eventually moved back to Ireland, but his most lasting studio records for Warner Brothers—**Astral Weeks** (1968), **Moondance** (1970), **Tupelo Honey** (1971), **St. Dominic's Preview** (1972), **Veedon Fleece** (1974), and **Into the Music** (1979)—dramatize the tension between Morrison's deep roots in Irish art (William Butler Yeats and

James Joyce are clear sources) and his unbridled love for American music (the Band and **Basement Tapes**–era Bob Dylan in particular).

What Morrison emerged with was not a mixture (which is what U2 and many others have come up with), but something totally new—and unquestionably Irish. Sinéad and U2's Bono are two of the many Irish performers who invoke the name of Van Morrison frequently and in reverential tones. One British band, Dexy's Midnight Runners, tried to pass itself off as Irish to claim Morrison's heritage; one Irish band, the Waterboys, released an album (**Fisherman's Blues**) that was a noble attempt to recreate for itself some of the power of **Astral Weeks**. For his part, Morrison recorded an album with the traditional-oriented Chieftains (**Irish Heartbeat**, 1988) that brought it all back home in spite of its rampant sentimentality.

Although Morrison's influence on Irish bands is extensive, it is not pervasive: some well-known rock groups like Cactus World News (second-level U2) and the Undertones (passable power pop) proceeded as if Morrison never existed. Morrison is the only Irish performer before Sinéad to create something wholly new, yet so many Irish bands have romantic notions about following U2 into megaplatinum notoriety that it is impossible for them to achieve such originality. Too many of them (like the aforementioned Cactus World News) acted as if aping a favored sound (say, U2's) was the same thing as expanding from it. In the end, they bore the same relationship to U2's music that the Knack did to the Beatles. Rootlessness, not always a bad thing, had been supplanted by crass opportunism.

Although nothing can tell the story of Irish rock and roll as sublimely as Morrison's records, two books try, and one nearly pulls it off. Mark J. Prendergast's **The Isle of Noises: Rock and Roll's Roots in Ireland** is a boosterish, excitable work with mostly good research, but throughout the volume Prendergast is too exhausted from revealing another trivial note about, say, some forgotten pub-rock group from Dublin that he never gets around to placing his factoids into context. He describes Sinéad's voice as "pure as the driven snow." As opposed to what: yellow snow?

Much more useful to an understanding of the Irish rock scene is Roddy Doyle's comic novel **The Commitments**, which dissects the brief, poignant career of a fictional Dubliner soul-revival band of the same name. The Commitments latch on to the soul music of Sam Cooke and Otis Redding because it sounds more "real" than what they hear in the local pubs and on the radio, and with the fanaticism of the newly converted (much like U2 in the United States during the **Rattle and Hum** sessions) they succeed marvelously, for example altering James Brown's "Night Train" so that the listed cities make sense on their island. "No one laughed," Doyle writes of one performance. "It wasn't funny. It was true." Of course the next second the band members are trading insults. At the end of the novel, the few members who haven't scattered are organizing a country-punk unit. They are just as committed to the new sound as they were to the old and their infatuation is contagious. They truly love their new toys, mid-1960s Byrds albums, but the reader is left with the hunch that six weeks later they might be playing power-pop polkas.

This is why it is so hard pinpointing the roots of Irish rock-and-roll bands, because those acquired roots could be different every few months. Had In Tua Nua with Sinéad lasted, they could have just as easily developed into a heavy-metal band as a full-fledged folkie outfit. There were paths open in all directions.

Sinéad did not remain long with In Tua Nua. Her father prevented her from touring with the group (listening to the music suggests she did not miss much), and that is when she wound up in Waterford. While at that boarding school, she worked harder on her music and began playing in public more regularly, usually in pubs or coffeehouses (often with a supporting guitarist). Bob Dylan covers were the rule, and early versions of **The Lion and the Cobra**'s artier tracks "Drink Before the War" and "Never Get Old" also got aired out. She lasted at Waterford roughly a year, after which time she decided she was going to make her living as a singer. At her father's urging, Sinéad studied briefly at Dublin's College of Music.

When she was seventeen, Sinéad joined a group called Ton Ton Macoute, as its singer. She was not allowed to write for the band. Nobody who has seen Ton Ton Macoute has anything positive to say about them (they did not stay together long enough to develop into anything worthy praising), and that was also the opinion of representatives of England's Ensign Records when they came to a Dublin rehearsal studio to audition several bands. They were impressed by none of them. Ensign's Nigel Grainge and Chris Hill were, however, taken by Sinéad's presence and intensity (though not by the songs she performed) and encouraged her. At that time Sinéad was still painfully shy in front of an audience—and doubly so before an audience made up of two British record-company executives—and Grainge and Hill could see that she would not be saleable unless she became more comfortable in public. Work on it, they told her, and we will be happy to hear you again. Uttering this half-inspiring, half-typical record-company blow-off, they returned to England.

Barely a month later (during which time Ton Ton Macoute quietly dissolved), a more confident Sinéad was convinced that she had grown enough to justify a record deal and wrote Grainge telling him as much. She alluded to Grainge's promise to help her record demos (demonstration versions of songs for reference use) and wrote that she was ready to come to England. Grainge's pledge to pay for her demos existed only in Sinéad's mind, but she was an ambitious kid who demanded she be heard. Like most rock-and-roll performers with brains, Sinéad has subsequently expressed serious reservations about success. But then, like most who have not tasted the downside of fame, she was hungry for it: she wanted what she did not have. Grainge, tickled by her audacity, sent the precocious Sinéad a plane ticket and promptly forgot about her.

On the inside of its June 14, 1990, cover story on Sinéad, **Rolling Stone** ran a photograph of her at Dublin Airport before she left for Great Britain. Sinéad still has a full head of straight black hair, she is wearing a denim jacket, and her luggage is on the floor between her legs. She stands straight, looks toward the camera, and reveals the slightest hint of a smile. She appears confident and worried at the same time. Then you notice that she is looking past the camera, imagining her future. She has no time for this moment; she has already moved on.

When Sinéad showed up at Ensign's office, a surprised Grainge sat her down and telephoned Karl Wallinger, one of the performers on his roster. North Wales native Wallinger, formerly of the Waterboys, was in London piecing togeth-er a solo project (which he released under the monicker World Party), and Grainge instructed him to lead young Sinéad through the rigors of recording her first professional-level demo tape.

Soon after, Grainge arrived at the demo studio, met a beaming Wallinger, and saw and heard Sinéad record a slashing version of ''Troy,'' a riveting announcement of pain in the wake of sexual treachery. (The other three songs she recorded that day were "Jerusalem," "Drink Before the War," and "Just Call Me Joe.") The stark performance, just Sinéad's supple voice and her entry-level guitar, set off an avalanche of terror that surprised both Grainge and Wallinger. Grainge committed immediately when he heard the four demos; Sinéad signed to Ensign Records and moved to London (a cold-water flat in Stoke-Newington) for good.

3

London

Sinéad remembers her years in London, woodshedding and writing **The Lion and the Cobra**, as lonely ones. As Ensign's Grainge told **Rolling Stone**'s Mikal Gilmore, "She spent a lot of time hanging around the [Ensign] office, making tea and answering phones." She had nothing else to do, nowhere else worthwhile to go.

Yet these were two years of remarkable musical growth for her. She developed her wan folk songs into full-fledged pieces and by mid-1986 she was ready to record them. Satisfied, Grainge and Hill were preparing to send her into the studio with producer Mick Glossop.

Two men Sinéad met during this period made a lasting impact on her. While in London, she found herself orbiting in the same circles as Fachtna O'Ceallaigh, a fellow Irishman with boundless rock ambitions. Several years earlier O'Ceallaigh had enjoyed a taste of rock success as manager of the Boomtown Rats and Bananarama, and he was as hungry to manage a platinum-plated act as Sinéad was hungry to be that act. O'Ceallaigh comes from the "personal" school of rock managers, believing in his clients with all his soul and doing all he can to protect his charge from real or imagined threats. O'Ceallaigh was the sort of manager that performers tend to love and everyone else tends to hate. Grainge, who had dealt with O'Ceallaigh in the Boomtown Rats' early days when they were signed to Ensign, all but ordered Sinéad not to sign up with O'Ceallaigh. For Sinéad, who wanted a strong manager, this was the heartiest recommendation O'Ceallaigh could have earned. O'Ceallaigh believed in her as strongly as Sinéad believed in herself; she trusted him.

Aside from being able to keep the executives at Ensign off-guard and away from Sinéad, O'Ceallaigh had something else going for him: connections. U2 had taken some of the money generated by their platinum album **The Unforgettable Fire** and the sold-out tour behind it and invested it in their own vanity label, Mother Records, designed to help fellow Irish bands who deserved a wide audience. O'Ceallaigh ran Mother Records.

Most such imprints are a nearly inevitable trapping of rock superstardom: the Beatles' Apple, Prince's Paisley Park, Rolling Stones, David Byrne's Fly and Luaka Bop. Even a second-tier star like Sting briefly had his own. It is worth nothing that none of these labels ever survive over the long haul (the few that do, like Paisley Park or Rolling Stones, are not real record labels, just an excuse to put a different logo on a product). Like most such labels, Mother Records was formed by U2 with a specific goal in mind. Record companies built on such narrow visions never succeed.

Although U2 should be lauded for wanting to invest some of their earnings into the scene that launched them, there was no way that such a plan could last. Even worse, the first group U2 chose to champion on Mother was

Cactus World News, a wildly derivative unit whose relationship to U2 was similar to that of John Cafferty and the Beaver Brown Band to Bruce Springsteen: an empty shadow of the real thing.

At the time, none of this mattered to O'Ceallaigh. He was in tight with U2, the most popular band in Ireland, and the most important pop performers on the island who were not Van Morrison. A head taller than Sinéad, O'Ceallaigh was a manager she was ready to look up to—and learn from.

The other important man who entered Sinéad's life in her pre-album London period was her future husband, John Reynolds. He was recruited as the drummer for Sinéad's debut record, and although his strongest credit was as stick man for Transvision Vamp, a British version of second-generation American punks Holly and the Italians, Reynolds fit in snugly with the studio group Sinéad and O'Ceallaigh were putting together. Something else must have clicked: Reynolds and Sinéad began dating soon after he joined the band.

But before she was to enter a studio to record her high-pressure debut album, nineteen-year-old Sinéad had one other project: a collaboration with a member of O'Ceallaigh's associates, U2. The band's guitarist, Dave Evans (known professionally as "the Edge"), was writing the soundtrack for a film called **The Captive** and wanted one of the tracks in this solo project to have a vocal. (U2 singer Paul "Bono" Hewson was a Sinéad fan as far back as In Tua Nua's "Take My Hand.") Sinéad flew to Dublin, O'Ceallaigh made the introduction, and Evans and Sinéad soon began collaborating. It is no exaggeration to label the track they wrote together, "Heroine" (no relation to the Velvet Underground song with the homonymous title), as a herculean leap above anything Sinéad had achieved with In Tua Nua or Ton Ton Macoute. For the first time she was working with someone at least her equal as a writer and performer. Sinéad would go on to become as much of a control freak as Prince, but there is no denying that a strong collaborator will force even the most insular rock performer to work harder. On "Heroine," Sinéad had finally found someone worthy of sharing her talent.

"Heroine" is built around synthesizers, but the warm sound of these electronic keyboards is an affront to the contrived, soul-free high-tech synthesizers of mid-eighties chart-toppers like Eurythmics. The first word out of Sinéad's mouth is "Afraid," and she pauses for a moment after those initial syllables, as if to suggest that this word is all she needs to say. (This is like the introductory line of Roy Orbison's "It's Over": "Your baby doesn't love you anymore." What more needs to be said?) But Sinéad's wistful voice is surrounded by instruments that cushion her more and more with each measure, and she can move on. As with much of Evans's music for U2, "Heroine" is a mood piece, evocation taking precedence over linear narrative. Lyrics do not add up to much, but Sinéad's performance of them is what matters. Her melismatic cry of "Bring me into your arms again," followed by one of Evans's trademark elliptical guitar lines, is at once affecting and provocative. This ballad never rushes its tempo but keeps building up steam; Sinéad sings free and hints at the multi-octave range she would soon explore in detail. Forget soundtrack music: "Heroine" was a formidable pop tune without any visuals to support it. It was an auspicious debut for Sinéad, recording for the first time under her own name; those who heard the song clamored for a full record by her.

Evans was so pleased by this recording that he invited Sinéad to open up for U2 at a special Belfast taping of the British pop-music television show the "Old Grey Whistle

Test." Though short, slim, and unknown, she surprised the audience with her all-encompassing voice, her stories of treachery, and her authority. She also surprised the audience because she was bald.

Not only had Sinéad experimented with her music in London, but she had also experimented with her hair. Ensign employees used to try to guess what she would come up with the next time she visited the office. (At the same time, Ensign officials also used to tease her that she sounded like a variety of other singers—Grace Slick, Aretha Franklin, Tammi Terrell—none of whom Sinéad said she had ever heard of, let alone heard.) After the usual user-hostile punk-influenced styles, Sinéad tried a Mohawk, quickly tired of the Mr. T. look, and moved on to a crew cut, and finally shaved off the remaining fuzz. Her bald pate—at once both provocative and strangely enticing—remains her focal point: as late as 1990, late-night talk-show mannequin Arsenio Hall still refers to her as "that little bald lady."

When **SPIN** magazine published its fifth anniversary issue in April 1990 it put Sinéad on the cover and ran a two-year-old interview (a typical **SPIN** device) Sinéad underwent with one of the magazine's senior editors, Legs McNeil. The article turned out to be more about McNeil than the interview subject (another normal **SPIN** strategy) and included one delightful piece of mythmaking that would be wonderful if it were true. According to that article, Sinéad's record company wanted her to "tart" up her image and present herself in a more "girlie" fashion, so she cut off all her hair. The truth is that Sinéad pulverized her hair for her own reasons, among them that she did not want to be another typical female rock star with big hair. All evidence suggests that she did it for herself, not as a response to someone else's unreasonable demands. Everyone had their own theory on why Sinéad cut her hair—ranging from she fell asleep in the barber's chair to she was serving public penance for some infidelity to some unnamed person—but none of these hypotheses ever came close to ringing true. Sinéad once said, apparently unaware of the charming self-contradiction, "Hair's a fashion statement and I don't want to make one."

The energetic bald woman entered a London studio to record **The Lion and the Cobra** with one more surprise: she was pregnant with her and Reynold's child. Encouraged by Reynolds and Ensign officials, Sinéad planned to have an abortion—she even got as far as the hospital—but made an eleventh-hour decision against it. Her life was in turmoil. She was pregnant by a man she clearly cared for but had not known for very long and as a result she did not know whether they would have a future together. She was living in London, a cold, big city whose chilliness and size exacerbated her loneliness and homesickness. She was also under the extreme pressure that comes with recording one's debut album.

Many pop performers obsess about their first major work, operating under the (alas, very likely) suspicion that if they do not score a hit the first time out they may not get another chance. This may be the only chance I ever get to garner an audience, they think, so I will simply shut myself off from everything else in my life and concentrate on the work. With her personal and professional problems as intense as they were at the time (as Ensign's Grainge suspected, O'Ceallaigh was beginning to drive a wedge between Sinéad and her record company), Sinéad had no such luxury. She could not lose herself in her work; the demands of real life were too pressing and could not be ignored.

Under those circumstances, it comes as little surprise that the sessions Sinéad recorded under producer Glossop's direction in the fall of 1986 were a bust. She was nervous, she and Glossop were frequently at odds on how the record was supposed to sound, and she was rounder by the day. Sinéad had not yet developed enough to be able to completely channel her problems into her music, and even if she had been able to, Glossop was viewed by both Sinéad and O'Ceallaigh as a patronizing impediment to making the record Sinéad and O'Ceallaigh wanted. When recording was completed and Glossop was ready to mix the record for release, Ensign officials finally agreed with Sinéad and O'Ceallaigh and decided to let Sinéad start from scratch and call the shots herself. She understood the songs better than anyone else; she would produce herself, with engineer Kevin Moloney aiding her on technical matters.

Sinéad must have gained some strength during this time, because she was able to produce a coherent album under tremendous stress. She started recording in April 1987, at which point she was nearly seven months pregnant and knew she had to get the project completed within two months. That she was able to pull this off at only twenty years of age is in some ways far more impressive than the record itself. That June, she completed the record (Ensign officials were as pleased with the results as she and O'Ceallaigh) and gave birth to a son, Jake Reynolds. Soon after Jake was born, she and John had a falling-out and she slid even closer to O'Ceallaigh.

4

The Lion
and the Cobra

Sinéad O'Connor

the
Lion

and

the
Cobra.

*T*ranslated from Gaelic, the hand-written inner sleeve of Sinéad's debut album reads: "You will tread upon the lion and the cobra. You will trample the great lion and the serpent." Sinéad may insist that she shies away from self-promotion, but such a sleeve note is a wonderful *chutzpah* gesture that shows that she knows she is great, and she will not rest until everyone knows it. (The fact that the note was in Gaelic also made sure that too many people were not in on the plan.) There are many quiet songs on **The Lion and the Cobra** but there is nothing polite about the nine-cut collection.

This is especially true of its cover photograph, in which Sinéad leans her head forward—drawing attention to her bare hint of hair—and grabs the straps of her shirt for support. She looks down at the ground, deep in tortured thought. Look closer and you will notice that Sinéad had scribbled an illegible note on the back of her left hand. The cover of **The Lion and the Cobra** announces that this record will be nothing like you have ever heard or seen before. The photograph depicts Sinéad as a contradiction: someone in some sort of pain, yet someone who is going to talk to an audience in a new way.

Indeed, for all but a few tracks, **The Lion and the Cobra** is an album sung by a confident woman who nonetheless needs frequent reassurance. She may stare at the camera with the intensity befitting a spiritual child of Johnny Rotten and she may wear the Doc Marten boots favored by the new generation of right-wing English punks (who, of course, are also skinheads, but that is where the similarities end), but that image is at odds with the vulnerable woman who sings the songs on **The Lion and the Cobra**. The image is one thing; the art is another.

Sinéad's core band for the record, aside from herself on vocals and guitar, and Reynolds on drums and drum programming, was made up of keyboardist Mike Clowes, guitarist Rob Dean, and bassist "Spike" Hollifield. (The most significant addition was Marco Pirroni, the former foil to Adam Ant, who overdubbed several guitars onto the album's only traditional hard-rock song, "Mandinka," and supercharged it.) Yet **The Lion and the Cobra** is very much an album by a solo artist, not a band album. Sinéad's voice and rhythm guitar are always upfront in the airy mix and, except for star-turn spoken cameos, no other voices are heard on the record. Many of the songs on **The Lion and the Cobra** have a big sound, but they are always traceable back to a solitary woman and her guitar.

The stark opening cut "Jackie" sets the agenda and exemplifies what is startling about **The Lion and the Cobra** and what remains unfinished. Her voice starts alone, beginning the tale of long-lost love, and a processed electric guitar mimicking strings gradually gains equal footing. It is an ominous mixture, and one that allows Sinéad to conjure up a wintry Gothic scene worthy of a narrator expressing an obsessive love for someone who has been "lying dead for twenty years." Her experimental singing is unprecedented in its switching between ethereal and harsh earthly voices—the song shows off her vocal strengths without resorting to the usual showoff moves of singers with broad ranges. Nonetheless the performance loses some of its conviction when Sinéad's roars of "Jackie" deteriorate into "Jackie O" chants. Aside from the celebrity angle (the last time JFK's widow appeared in a pop song was Tim Curry's name-dropping "I Do the Rock" and Human Sexual Response's "I Want to Be Jackie Onassis,"), the move diminishes the intimate effect Sinéad is after.

There are no such problems with "Mandinka." Its combination of torrid vocals and great crunchy guitars rocked hard enough to satisfy the programmers at American album-oriented radio stations, yet its concerns were so different from those of the usual AOR longhair boys that the track stood out immediately. The three guitarists (Sinéad, Dean, and Pirroni) gnaw at their riffs while Sinéad's heavily processed voice screams. In the chorus she sings with a full throat, "I don't know no shame/I feel no pain/I can't/ See the flame." Remarkably, she slips in a subtle pause between singing the third and fourth lines, lending a fruitful double meaning (toward the end of the song, Sinéad underlines this point by singing the passage without the fourth line). Sung by a twenty-year-old bald, unmarried, pregnant woman convinced that she is somehow different from others, these lines are penetrating and persuasive.

"Mandinka" shows how Sinéad can work with well-worn materials and come up with something new. The pivotal lines are far from unprecedented: "I'm not the same/I have no shame" Madonna sang on her debut

album's "Burnin' Up," albeit in a significantly more con-
strained context (lust is only one of the many concerns of
the outgoing "Mandinka"). The electric-guitar chords of
"Mandinka" are worthy of a first-rate heavy-metal group
like AC/DC; Sinéad sharpens her lyrical point but smooths
her sound by grating acoustic guitars atop "Mandinka's"
snow slide of electric guitars. The interaction between
acoustic and electric is a canny mirror to the vulnerable
and aggressive aspects of Sinéad's vinyl presence. When
she reaches the song's soothing repeated lyrical tag, "So I
can give you my heart," she tempers her caustic side but
still sounds powerful. A complex mixture of all that made
Sinéad interesting, "Mandinka" is a terrific single that
repays repeated listenings with newfound pleasures.

The Lion and the Cobra is a debut album full of songs
written by Sinéad when she was still a teenager, and as a
result the young performer and writer is not able to
maintain the intensity of "Mandinka" throughout the
record. Yet even the songs that do not survive inspection
reveal much about Sinéad and some of them even set the
stage for future triumphs. "Jerusalem" has some supple
riffing and Sinéad delivers a nearly funky performance
subverted by her overly arch and poetic words. As "Jackie"
also showed, "Jerusalem" offers evidence that Sinéad has
not yet perfected a voice that can show agitation without
sounding whiny. "Jerusalem" also loses itself in a cluttered
sound—its adventurous middle section sounds like a col-
lage of sound effects.

"Just Like U Said It Would B" is on the same level. Its
folkie introduction leans on **Rubber Soul**–era Beatles guitar, and its tale of yet another religious rite of passage (it is
unclear if its sarcastic tone depicts spiritual or sexual
deflowering) remains unformed. Couplets like "Will you be
my lover/Will you be my mama" reveal nothing except

the transported manner in which Sinéad pushes them across. Still, "Just Like U Said It Would B" marries British folk (in the tradition of the groundbreaking folk-rock group Fairport Convention) with the updated-Baroque stylings of the Left Banke during a lengthy journey worth taking at least once.

The self-consciously arty "Never Get Old" is more problematic. Its elevated tone diffuses a good hook, reminiscent of **Aja**-period Steely Dan, that appears once Reynolds's drums finally kick in hard against Sinéad's wordless moans. What sidetracks the song the most is the cameo of arty Irish singer Enya (full name: Enya Ní Bhronáin). Enya's Gaelic-language spoken sections serve as intentionally elitist devices, because they make sure that most fans will not be able to understand what is going on; the vast majority of Sinéad's audience will miss out on part of the story. Such elitism is expected from arty bohemians (Enya's music and the tape-looped moans of "Never Get Old" reside in Laurie Anderson's land of "O Superman"), but it has nothing to do with the direct emotional communication Sinéad is trying for throughout **The Lion and the Cobra**.

Covering similar elevated musical territory to "Never Get Old" and "Jackie" but much more successful and engaging is the next track, the six-and-one-half-minute-long psychodrama "Troy." An outstanding dissection of the treacherous journey from love to betrayal, "Troy" marries wide-screen sound to an expansive tale that takes in small domestic moments and grand ones derived from Greek mythology with equal finesse (although Sinéad's promise that "I'd kill a dragon for you/And die" is a bit much). Synthesized strings nudge along Sinéad as she gets to the heart of a relationship destroyed by lies. She addresses the song to her unfaithful lover, and you can feel him squirm, although the narrator seems too entrenched in her own pain to notice.

Except for the occasional lyrical cliché (there are several phoenixes rising from flames in this song), "Troy" is an ideal showcase for showing how closely Sinéad can focus on affairs of the heart. The version of "Troy" on **The Lion and the Cobra** has since been overtaken by the sparse live version that Sinéad performs alone with an acoustic guitar and climaxes with the spat-out scream, "You're still a fucking liar," but this is not some demure singer-songwriter scolding an ex-lover; its pretensions notwithstanding, it feels real.

Such ghosts cannot be exorcised over and over, so Sinéad follows "Troy" with "I Want Your (Hands on Me)," a savvy white-girl funk exercise. It is an urgent song that is full of demands for physical affection and promises of what will happen if the listener takes her up on her offer. Electric guitars bounce off Reynolds's programmed drum patterns, leaving plenty of room for Sinéad to spray lust in all directions. She feeds the rhythm, and she in turn draws strength from the rhythm.

(Incidentally, both "I Want Your [Hands on Me]" and "Mandinka" sound much hotter than the rest of **The Lion and the Cobra**, probably because they were remixed by different people after the initial mix by producer Sinéad, engineer Moloney, and manager O'Ceallaigh. The quieter songs on **The Lion and the Cobra** gradually insinuate themselves into the listener's consciousness; "I Want Your [Hands on Me]" and "Mandinka" are in your face from the moment they begin.)

The Lion and the Cobra does not sound like a record U2 would make—there is little connection here to her countrymates' "Three Chords and the Truth" aesthetic— but it is certainly as dour and straight-faced as U2 at its most serious and sacred-minded. Instead of digging into the story and searching for details that will enhance it, Sinéad plows straight ahead into unencumbered declaration. And like U2 at its best, Sinéad is usually committed enough to the emotions of the song that its lack of concrete details does not matter nearly as much as the sweep of the music.

The Lion and the Cobra winds down with two of its oldest compositions. "Drink Before the War" is a smoldering ballad in which Sinéad imagines herself as a soldier on the brink of battle. Most of the rhymes are too easy ("You live in a shell/Create your own hell"; "You dig your own grave/It's a life you can save"). But when two-thirds into the organ-driven track Sinéad casts aside the rhetoric and lets the song tell the vivid story of lives breaking apart, the earlier lyrical gaffes do not seem as bothersome. "Drink Before the War" features perhaps Sinéad's slyest singing on the record, all purposeful swoops and asides.

The record slides out on "Just Call Me Joe," a feedback-heavy ballad built around the ominous fret work of guest guitarist Kevin Mooney, who wrote the song under the pseudonym Black Moon E. When Sinéad kicks off the song by announcing "We came here across the Great Divide," it is easy to fear that "Just Call Me Joe" will blather bland, grand myths for six minutes, but the harsh, fuzz-toned guitar lines, derived from Lou Reed's Velvet Underground druggy laments and Neil Young's minor-keyed Crazy Horse epics, overwhelm and then slash through any problems in the lyrics.

"Just Call Me Joe" is a barbed, yet ironically low-key ending to an album that as a whole is anything but low-key. **The Lion and the Cobra** immediately established Sinéad as an Irish visionary in the tradition of Van Morrison, worthy of all the anticipation built up by her song on the **Captive** soundtrack. Sinéad had lived up to the liner-note boast: she had tread on the lion and the cobra, and emerged from that experience wiser and more ferocious.

But such an emotionally penetrating album is not what usually yields hit records (ask anyone from Richard Thompson to Steve Earle). The American arm of Sinéad's label projected sales of only twenty-five thousand, and some in the company did not even think that Sinéad, a woman they perceived to be quite odd, would get even that far.

Sinéad's debut album arrived in unsuspecting record stores at a time when albums by female pop performers were considered an amusing novelty. Retrogressive folk-oriented performers like Suzanne Vega and Tracy Chapman were all the rage for young fans who had missed Joni Mitchell the first time around and for older fans who simply missed her. For no other reason than because she was a woman, Sinéad was lumped in with these overt folkies. She commented on it best herself in an interview with Bill Coleman that ran in **Musician**. "I'm not an admirer of folk music, of Suzanne Vega and Joni Mitchell," she said. "All that stuff is wishy-washy as far as I'm concerned." Yet because she happened to be a woman whose diverse music had some folk elements, it was easy to pigeonhole her. (Other female performers, less famous than Sinéad but no less gifted, such as Sam Phillips, were similarly rounded up and ghettoized.) Many trees were cut down to support the musings of journalists who wanted to ponder what it all meant and make great pronouncements about it.

What it all meant was simple: one female folkie, Suzanne Vega, had one number three single with "Luka," an electrified song that Vega says is about child abuse but may really be about wife-beating. Whatever the case, "Luka" was a fluke female folkie hit, and instead of taking it on as the isolated case it was, the music industry decided that it was a trend. So an avalanche of articles about "Women in Rock" appeared, as if that were a legitimate category. Why didn't anybody run an article about "Men in Rock," featuring Pete Townshend, Boy George, and Robert Cray, since they had as much (as little) in common as the women in those roundup pieces? Alas, the reason is that the music industry has a rich history of sexism. Of the dozens of unmatchable rock performers, few are women. And those few are usually controlled by men, as Ike Turner's former wife Tina would be happy to tell you. **TV Guide** once ran a cover story with the lying title, "Why Women Now Rule Rock." The three women it showcased on the cover—Janet Jackson, Paula Abdul, and Madonna—were female performers who, however feisty, conformed to traditional male expectations of what a lady pop singer should be like. Sinéad was not on the cover, nor were any female rappers; the women that **TV Guide** claimed ruled rock were the women whom men wanted to do the ruling, because they knew it would be a safe rule.

To the broad rock audience (and by extension the rock industry), rock and roll has always meant rock and roll written and recorded by men. It is impossible for many to imagine a female equivalent of Jerry Lee Lewis, Jimi Hendrix, or David Bowie, because we do not think of them as male performers—simply as rockers. There are no major nonperforming female record producers. When the occasional woman does attempt to be a hard rocker on male hard-rock terms—be she Joan Jett or Patti Smith—she is greeted as if she were a freak.

This is as true of race as it is of sex. When the hard-rock

quartet Living Color released its debut album in 1988, newspapers and magazines were filled with stories about "black rock and roll," which was obscene, since nearly all rock and roll is descended from forms originated by African-Americans, and "black rock and roll" should have been considered a redundant term. But racial polarization in the United States had reached such a fever pitch by the end of the second Reagan administration that the idea of African-Americans playing rock and roll had become a novelty.

Under these circumstances, there was no way that Sinéad could be received as what she was: a talented young performer with provocative looks and sounds. There was no existing structure under which the pop-music industry could handle a "bald chick." So instead of trying to figure out Sinéad, the industry tried to assimilate her.

5

America

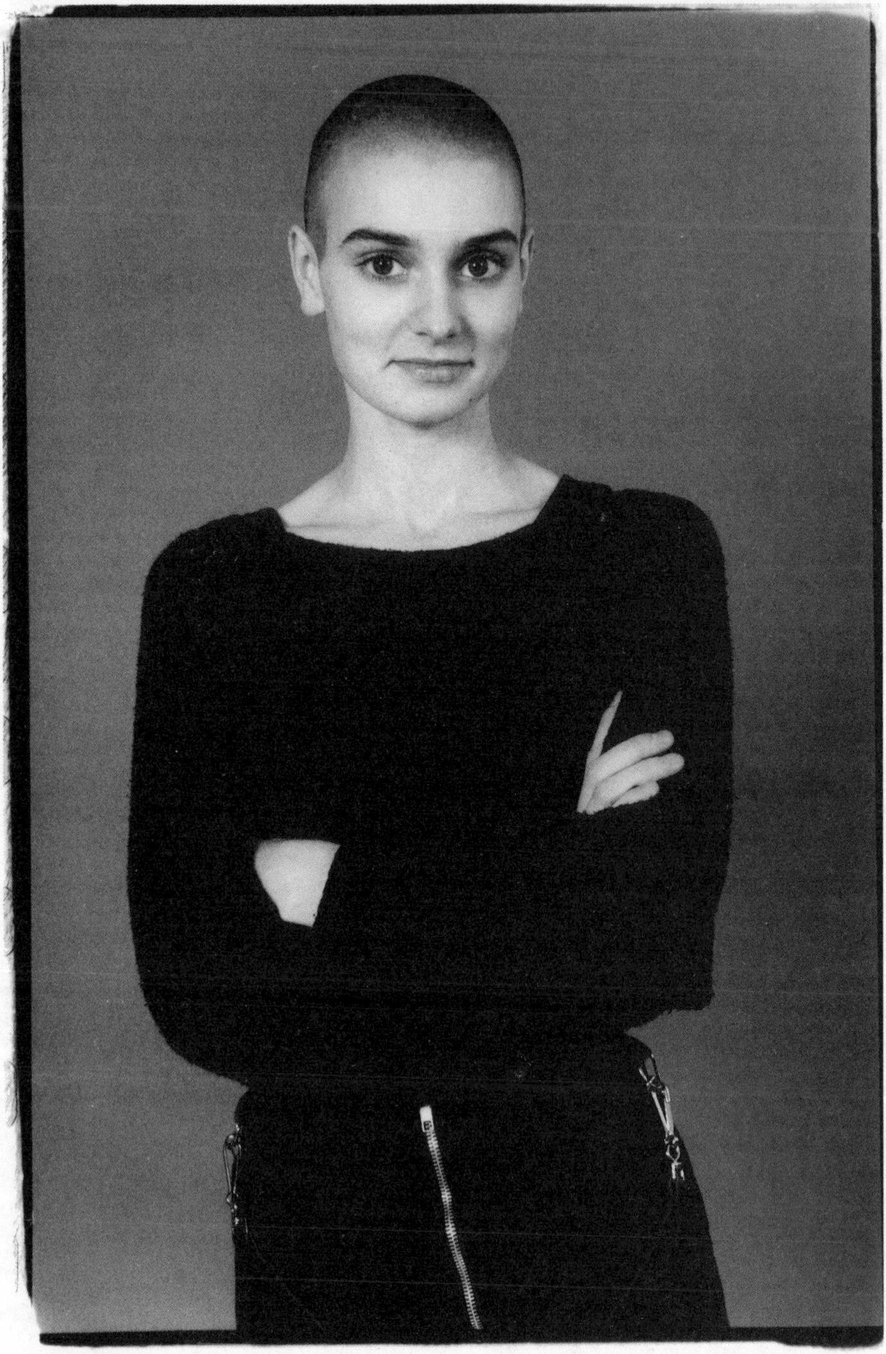

Laura Levine

*T*he clumsy, knee-jerk attempts by the music industry to place the round head of Sinéad into a preformed square hole only strengthened the young woman's growing resolve. Sinéad may have had a big mouth when she sang, but that was going to be nothing compared to what she could do with it when she talked.

Before Sinéad could get out the good word about herself, she had to deal with a new record company. Ensign had hammered out a distribution deal with Chrysalis, who would market **The Lion and the Cobra** internationally. But a shortage of cash at Ensign led to a deal in which the company of Nigel Grainge and Chris Hill became a wholly owned subsidiary of Chrysalis. The division still had autonomy to sign whatever artists it wished, and its small roster of Sinéad, World Party, the Waterboys, and the Blue Aeroplanes was distinctive and impressive, successful both artistically and commercially. But for all intents and purposes, Sinéad was considered by Chrysalis employees and outsiders alike as a Chrysalis performer.

Grainge and Hill sometimes complained that Chrysalis head Mike Bone (and his successor John Sykes) did not emphasize Ensign's important place in the Sinéad package, but the Ensign pair had to admit that, especially in the United States, Chrysalis was a more likely vehicle for breaking their acts big time. Chrysalis was going through some hard times—longtime stalwart Pat Benatar was not having hits anymore with her usual frequency and meal-ticket soft-rockers Huey Lewis and the News were about to leave the label.

Still, Chrysalis had some unexpected recent success with Billy Idol, a punk poseur with a sneer stolen from Sid Vicious and an AOR by-the-numbers sound that Vicious would have deplored. Idol, a British punk veteran (he sang for the extremely minor punk band Generation X, which also spawned the founder of the even more useless Sigue Sigue Sputnik), was inexplicably considered to have some hip cachet, so the feeling was that if Chrysalis could break Idol, they might also be able to break Sinéad.

Also in Chrysalis's favor as far as Sinéad was concerned was that they worked hard on Karl Wallinger's World Party debut, **Private Revolution**, and culled from it two radio hits: the title track (with a video that featured Sinéad beating on a drum) and "Ship of Fools," a sturdy tale of ecological doom chanted over a precise **Beggar's Banquet**— era Rolling Stones rhythm track. If Sinéad had to be on a major United States label—and she did if she wanted to sell more than ten thousand records—there were many worse choices than Chrysalis. For example, it was unlikely that shmoozemeisters CBS Records president Walter Yetnikoff or MCA Records' Irving Azoff would have had a clue as to what to do with a female performer who did not succumb to convention at the first request.

No doubt around the same time he was getting used to

working for Chrysalis, Grainge also rolled his eyes over the latest predicament in which his once-again nemesis, Sinéad manager Fachtna O'Ceallaigh, had found himself. (Grainge would have continued to badmouth O'Ceallaigh to Sinéad if O'Ceallaigh had not made it extremely difficult for those two to meet without O'Ceallaigh there.) The colorful Fachtna had talked himself out of his job running Mother Records.

O'Ceallaigh advocated a virulent stand in favor of Sinn Fein, the political arm of the Irish-separatist terrorist organization, the Irish Republican Army. This stand had alienated him from the just-as-virulently pacifist members of U2. In the film **Rattle and Hum**, Bono precedes an incendiary "Sunday Bloody Sunday" by relating how people in the United States of Irish descent often expected him to take up the armed struggle against the British. Bono's onstage retort is, "Fuck the revolution!" In this context, O'Ceallaigh's *"Vive le révolution"* attitude was nothing less than anathema.

The boys in U2 loved O'Ceallaigh as a hard-ass character until he started working for them; eccentrics are always more enjoyable when they are not on the payroll. O'Ceallaigh hammered in a few more coffin nails when he told one reporter, "I literally despise the music that U2 make." When he was sacked, Sinéad, being a client and close friend of O'Ceallaigh, naturally took the side of her mentor, whom she thanked in the notes to **The Lion and the Cobra** as "my biggest influence and my best friend." It was a position that would one day cause her much sorrow.

In the interviews she granted to promote **The Lion and the Cobra**, Sinéad acted like any precocious twenty-year-old who had a microphone pushed in her face. She said things like, "I'm not concerned with being famous [but] with having a life," and gained instant respect, and unlike the respect the press had for her labelmate Billy Idol, this deference was not forced or given without thinking. Sinéad was good copy, and O'Ceallaigh encouraged her to dispense off-the-cuff provocative pronouncements off the top of the head that many interviewers could not help but stare at until she stopped them.

To the surprise of virtually everyone at Chrysalis, magazines were clamoring for interviews and people were buying the record. Chrysalis's projection of twenty-five thousand sales was quickly surpassed. Perhaps in penance for his lack of original belief (but more likely as a publicity gesture), Chrysalis president Bone shaved his head.

Even conservative commercial American radio was playing the record. Sinéad's beachhead on the United States airwaves was college radio (also known as "alternative radio") stations, which made sense. College radio has always been extremely open to performers who do not look mainstream—especially if that performer is mildly androgynous, and an apparently literate manipulator of obscure, angst-filled lyrics. Sinéad personified this category and was a natural on the alternative and college charts. What could be more *outré* to upper-middle-class American kids than a skinny bald lady with an Irish accent? But it must have been her success in the much larger AOR market that sent Bone to his razor.

The shock was that Sinéad did not fit in there with all the aging, mystic male rock stars. Frequent listeners of American album radio must operate under the fear that they are going to hear the same three songs over and over until they die of old age. Album radio peaked as an influence on the American record-buying public in the early 1970s, so it is not surprising that the format's few stalwart tracks date from that period. It is surprising that any United States resident with access to an FM radio would want to buy an album containing Lynyrd Skynyrd's "Free Bird," the Who's "Won't Get Fooled Again," Led Zeppelin's "Stairway to Heaven," or Blue Oyster Cult's "(Don't Fear) The Reaper" because it is only a slight exaggeration to suggest that AOR formats are a tape loop of those songs: all someone has to do to hear one of those songs is turn on the radio and wait a few minutes. The few more recent songs on the format—from groups like Foreigner and Winger—are so deeply grounded in the arena rock of the early 1970s that they might as well be by cover bands. The main reason rock radio lost significant market share in the 1980s—even more than added competition and the advent of narrowcasting—was that the playlists had not changed much in a decade. "Won't Get Fooled Again" is indeed a landmark, break-through rock song, but hearing the epic tune every few hours for fifteen years is enough to make even the most ardent Who fan scream in misery.

There was only one song on **The Lion and the Cobra** that could have squeezed into tight-listed AOR formats—"Mandinka"—and Chrysalis promotion people pushed the song hard to album-radio program directors after it had proved itself on college radio. Sometimes college-radio icons can make the move to AOR stardom, but that is the exception, not the rule. For every R.E.M. or Replacements, there are hundreds of Robyn Hitchcocks or Alarms. To make that jump from a market of one hundred thousand to a market of millions, one has to be distinct. Marco Pirroni's guitar chords chopped down hard enough for "Mandinka" to stand alongside the big boys, but what got the song on the radio cut even harder against the grain: Sinéad was different. Fans of rock radio were fed up, and they were open to someone whose music could fit in but who had an image that was a little more modern than the dinosaurs.

This difference was exploited in a tremendously effective publicity campaign engineered by Elaine Schock, a veteran record-company publicist who had just started her own company. It was a good mix; Schock is one of the few major rock publicists not based in a major city, and the distance from the industry insanity of New York or Los Angeles allowed for a less crazed orchestration of the campaign. Sinéad was Schock's first client; Schock had something to prove on her first free-lance job and her enthusiasm was essential to getting Sinéad's face in the press, which led to more interest on the part of radio programmers. Of course the only thing most disk jockeys could think to say over the air about Sinéad was that she had no hair; it was superficial DJ talk but it was publicity.

Live shows also helped sell the record. Although Sinéad and her band only toured through clubs and small halls, such intimate settings enhanced the quiet, insular songs that made up the bulk of **The Lion and the Cobra**. Her hour-plus sets featured most of the songs from her debut album, as well as a harsh, unrecorded tale called "The Value of Ignorance." She played several of the songs accompanied only by her guitar and in doing so did her best to minimize the inevitable distance between performer and audience. Although she had a relatively fast-selling album out of a major label, she did her best to recapture the coffeehouse atmosphere of her earliest performances. The most riveting of these solo acoustic tunes was her recasting of "Troy." Stripped of its ornamental orchestration, the hurt and ambivalence of the tune shone through. Only Sinéad and a guitar, this "Troy" nonetheless wailed. Many fans left these shows moved.

* * *

The Lion and the Cobra was not a hit of **I Do Not Want What I Haven't Got** proportions—it did not achieve platinum certification—but it was a sizable hit, eventually nudging past half a million sales in the United States alone. Aside from press, radio, and live performances, Sinéad was able to get across via music videos. Three of the songs from **The Lion and the Cobra**—"Troy," "I Want Your (Hands on Me)," and "Mandinka"—were filmed by John Maybury, and taken as a whole they outline the parameters of Sinéad's interests. Videos are for the most part mindless advertisements, and Sinéad's videos suffer from the usual problems inherent in the genre (an awkward mixture of the obvious, the overstated, and the overreaching), but the songs are too good to be ruined by forced images.

The film for "Troy" runs a full ten minutes and sixteen seconds, and takes in more than just that track. It's opening section includes much of "Never Get Old" and snatches of other tracks from **The Lion and the Cobra**; by the time it settles into "Troy," the viewer has been subjected to a barrage of images of Sinéad looking moody in a variety of situations. The visuals during the song proper are as extravagant as the musical arrangement: Sinéad is spun in a circle while in various bare-shouldered guises, one of them reminiscent of Pussy Galore's gold-painted sister who was murdered in **Goldfinger**. This was the first **The Lion and the Cobra** video to be released, and as such it introduced Sinéad in her defrocked-nun persona. She wears loose gowns, stares into the distance, and comes off like nothing more than the corresponding secretary of the Kate Bush fan club. The video is artier than the song and as such does not serve it well.

Much more assertive, at least, was the clip for "I Want Your (Hands on Me)," which also featured M. C. Lyte performing her brief rap from the twelve-inch-single version of the song. Sinéad wears a leather jacket and sways as images of flowers and hands race behind her. She stares boldly at the camera. At the same time she dares it to respond to her demand for physical affection and conveys that she is powerful enough to thrive even if she does not score. Again, some may have perceived her stares as aggressive, but they were simply the hallmarks of a confident woman.

Sinéad reinvented herself again in the video for "Mandinka." True rockers may have been disappointed that Sinéad did not present "Mandinka" for MTV viewers as the excellent straight-ahead guitar rocker she allowed it to be on record and in concert, but even with its quick cuts and reliance on twirling models, this is not nearly as arty as, say, the video version of "Troy." Sinéad lip-synchs "Mandinka," a crucifix earring dangling from her left ear, without calling attention to the energy and insistence of the tune. The camera lingers on her during the soothing coda rather than during the more dynamic earlier sections; if anything, this video seeks to downplay the song's aggressiveness.

Listening to **The Lion and the Cobra**, attending the tour supporting it, and watching the videos culled from it yield impressive evidence that anyone who considered Sinéad aggressive or pushy (or one of the sexist synonyms for such an attitude) was not paying attention to the performer's work. Every song Sinéad performed in 1987 and 1988 was built on the platform of the singer's vulnerability. Those who thought Sinéad came on too strong were responding to what she did outside the concert hall or the concert studio, and that is very different. Too many critics reviewed her interviews instead of her record, and they were reviewing a totally different type of performer.

The Sinéad who showed up for interviews lived up to the notice she received in the weekly British pop-music newspaper **New Musical Express**: "the female Johnny Rotten of the Nineteen Eighties, an angst-ridden young woman who shocked society with her looks and views." What could this tiny, vulnerable woman have done to justify comparisons to the singer of the Sex Pistols?

Pop-music performers who receive too much attention at too early an age tend to flip out. Michael Jackson became a zookeeper hermit; Prince became a sexual hermit; W. Axl Rose, of Guns n' Roses, verbalized, and then acted out, his most hateful fantasies. Sinéad looked at the phalanx of microphones before her and wanted to make noise. She wanted to be as articulate and confrontational as Bob Dylan and as concise and confrontational as Johnny Rotten. She may have been afraid to rock out in her music, but her chatter blared like a Jimi Hendrix guitar solo. No wonder the reporter from **People** magazine referred to her haircut as a "Manson-family" 'do; that is how intense and outrageous she was.

Sinéad encouraged the press to liken her childhood troubles to those of the Artful Dodger from Charles Dickens's **Oliver Twist**, and emphasized how one of the boarding schools she shuffled through was connected to a nursing home for terminal patients. "For punishment they would make us sleep on the floor in the old people's section," she told **People**. "There were rats everywhere, and the old women moaning and vomiting." She attacked aborted producer Mick Glossop at every opportunity, and tried to convince her audience that she was not a typical egotistical rock star ("I don't ever want to get in the position where I think I'm something special just because I wrote a damn song").

But Sinéad *was* something special, and she surely knew it. How else could she be so confident of her own opinions and be so willing to express them at the most tenuous provocation? Part of it was that as Sinéad turned twenty-one she was very much under the influence of the clique led by her manager O'Ceallaigh, and like most people of that age she parroted the beliefs of the people she wanted to impress. The other part of it was that, also like most twenty-one-year olds, she was in love with her own ideas.

She blames O'Ceallaigh for her statements from those days that she most regrets now. And her comments at the time about U2, its associates, and the general state of affairs in Ireland were clearly provoked by O'Ceallaigh's bitterness over being sacked as head of Mother Records by U2. Sinéad loved O'Ceallaigh, and she could not tolerate the attacks O'Ceallaigh told her were being launched against him. In **i-D**, she tore into U2's "bombastic" music. In **Melody Maker**, which is to the **New Musical Express** as **Time** is to **Newsweek**, she attacked Hothouse Flowers, a not-bad folk-tinged act on Mother, calling the band's singer a "poseur." Like a good punk, she was biting the hand that first fed her. U2 had been her earliest sponsor, but her former friend was now the enemy of her current friend, so U2 was now her enemy, too.

It was in that **Melody Maker** interview that Sinéad most clearly betrayed her naïveté about everything: interpersonal relationships, how the pop-music industry works, and the pure evil that propels many in the Irish Republican Army. Her crucial misstatement was: "I support the IRA and Sinn Fein. I don't like the violence but I do understand it even though it's terrible."

Such bravura came home to roost almost immediately. Sinéad was not talking for herself—she was talking in defense of O'Ceallaigh. In chastising U2 at the peak of their popularity, Sinéad felt the wrath of the group's fans in the British, Irish, and (to a lesser degree) American and Canadian music establishments. Finally, her comments about the Irish Republican Army were simply ignorant. Such quotes made good copy, but they worked against the very human qualities of her music. It was impossible to reconcile the music with the mouth, unless one considered either the music or the mouth to be a fake. Fortunately, it turned out to be the mouth that was fake.

At the time nobody knew this, not even Sinéad, who became more brazen with every opportunity. She was the female equivalent of her contemporary Terence Trent D'Arby, another mammothly gifted performer whose self-promotion was as effective as his music. But D'Arby was careful to be controversial about himself and let fans and critics worry about his raging ego while at the same time accepting that he was very intelligent; fans and critics of Sinéad were forced to worry whether she thought before she opened her mouth. O'Ceallaigh loved what she said; the executives at Chrysalis and Ensign let it go on because they perceived it as helping them to sell more copies of **The Lion and the Cobra**. In fact, there may have been some pressure on Sinéad (from record-company people as well as O'Ceallaigh) to be confrontational: it kept her unusual first name out where people saw and heard it, and it accentuated how Sinéad was different from the flock of female folk singers.

Sinéad climaxed her support of **The Lion and the Cobra** with a lip-synching performance at the Grammy Awards, one of the American music industry's many annual tributes to itself. The Grammy Awards are the official honors of the National Association of Recording Arts and Sciences, and as such bear little relation to what is really happening in pop music. Because it is controlled by industry honchos, it only recognizes acts that have been commercially successful. Winners are invariably platinum-plated veterans. The organization moves slowly to recognize change: it has frequently recognized the same performer for the identical record two years running, such as Paul Simon's **Graceland**. It once awarded a Grammy in the "Heavy Metal" category to Jethro Tull, a fatuous group only slightly more affiliated with heavy metal than the Beach Boys. The show is a procession of Oscar-style self-congratulation. Bald-headed and fierce-looking among the wide-smiled moussed stars, Sinéad was like "Twin Peaks" at television's Emmy Awards eighteen months later: she was miles ahead of everybody else, she had upset the status quo, and nobody knew quite what to do with her.

Although she had to contend with the stupidity that is lip-synching before a live performance (and she has never mentioned why she did not play live, as others did that night), Sinéad blazed through "Mandinka" as well as she could. Wearing an elaborate dark bra, a pair of ripped dungarees with a "Jake" patch on her knee and a strip of her son's clothing dangling from a belt loop, her trademark Doc Marten boots, and the logo for the rap group Public Enemy stenciled into her bald head, she made jaws drop from Washington to Florida.

Nothing can completely save a lip-synched live performance, but Sinéad's marvelous, iconoclastic rendition of "Mandinka" came as close as virtually anyone has. In the midst of the polite evening, she came on like a punk. For the first time she delivered a performance that lived up to her rhetoric. The audience (both live and in their homes) were stunned. They were not used to seeing something that appeared real. Flagrantly sexual, built on inside jokes (most people neither knew Jake nor Public Enemy), it was a performance that succeeded precisely because it did not belong.

Although Chrysalis's Mike Bone was thrilled to have placed Sinéad on such a widely viewed showcase, there were also rumblings in Chrysalis and Ensign that Sinéad had gone too far this time. **Variety** reported Nigel Grainge as saying, "We realize that she had turned off a lot of people that night." Quietly company officials began to discuss toning down their unlikely star, but everyone knew that was unlikely as long as Fachtna O'Ceallaigh remained her keeper.

The most daring element of Sinéad's Grammy appearance was probably her implicit endorsement of Public Enemy. Sinéad championed rap before it was cool—or, at least, expected—for a white singer to do so. Sinéad was always a rap fan from the moment she showed up; she picked Rob Base to open her American-debut show at the World in New York.

True aficionados of rap recognized that hip-hop culture had been for the most part struggling to find new ideas since the glory days of Afrika Bambaataa and Soul Sonic Force, Grandmaster Flash and the Furious Five, and Run-D.M.C. ended in 1984. But Public Enemy was one of the few interested in finding new barriers to break. Musically they were sublime: they could turn random less-than-one-second samples into original-sounding new hooks, and rappers Chuck D. and Flavor Flav were as resilient a straight-man-and-comic-foil team as pop music had ever seen. Politically they were incendiary: the group's ideology verged on racial separatism, and they had close ties to Louis Farrakhan, the Muslim minister whose worthwhile ideas about breaking the economic yokes of racism were dwarfed by his frequent outbursts of hatred. Public Enemy made great records, but Sinéad's seeming endorsement of the group made Sinéad-watchers wonder if once again she should have picked her friends more carefully.

By this time, Sinéad could not have cared less about such public considerations. After her Grammy performance, she flew back to London and married John Reynolds.

6

Control

*T*hose around Sinéad, many of them part of O'Ceallaigh's circle of Irish patriots, were more than flabbergasted when their meal ticket switched gears and married John Reynolds. She had spent the year since Jake's birth drifting away from Reynolds and closer to O'Ceallaigh. Nobody expected this.

There has been much speculation in the British tabloids, in more legitimate American magazines like **Musician**, and among Sinéad fans as to whether O'Ceallaigh was ever Sinéad's lover. Who cares? It is none of our business and it does not really matter. What really does matter is that Sinéad was going through what she felt was a difficult time and she became closer to one important person in her life while distancing herself from the other. The triangle of Sinéad, O'Ceallaigh, and Reynolds was certainly deeply emotional even if it was not necessarily sexual.

During an extended tour like Sinéad's 1988 foray, it is easy to romanticize domesticity. Unless one is selling out multiple nights at arenas or stadiums, allowing a leisurely pace that more closely approximates normal travel, touring in a rock-and-roll band can be a nomadic, tedious, and intermittently depressing existence. The standard Holiday Inn room turns into a prison cell after one has been in a dozen consecutive ones that look exactly the same; buses and vans turn into traveling prison cells or daily rides to hell (Woody Guthrie's "Bound for Glory" train in reverse); every town and stage looks the same; chest colds feel like tuberculosis; it is hard to tell what day it is unless one reads the local newspapers; no one and nothing is permanent; and dislocation is the only feeling that remains long enough to make an impact.

Rock bands write about this all the time, some with insight, most not. Longhair New Jersey knucklehead superstar Jon Bon Jovi has written what seems like ten thousand songs equating traveling rock bands with gunslingers on the run. Rather than traveling salesmen like Willy Loman, many rockers see themselves as searchers of truth rambling from town to town until they find some cosmic answer.

This existential longing is complete bullshit. Touring with a rock-and-roll band has its exhilarating moments, even a few enlightening moments if one is lucky, but there are also long stretches of tedium and normal interaction with people who are not musicians. In other words, except for the cocooned (and there are many who turn to a life of rock on the road because its fosters the most arrogant kind of dependence), rock touring is closer to real life than many are willing to admit.

Still, such a life necessitates staying away from home for decidedly long stretches, and there is something particularly unpleasant about that life for a parent of an infant, especially the female parent, on whom society frowns if she is away from her child. The lengthy travel periods, the hours between sound check and performance waiting for something to happen, and all the wide-space trappings of such an existence offer more than ample time for reflection about everything in a rocker's life. One can look at baby pictures only so long without needing to go home.

Sinéad took that time to think, and by the end of her tour she began to realize that her life was getting out of control. Moving back to London and marrying Reynolds was one way of starting to deal with the problem. Getting married also created some necessary friction between Sinéad and O'Ceallaigh. Necessary, that is, if Sinéad was going to become her own person.

Sinéad's work of this period is accurately documented by **The Value of Ignorance**, a short (only thirty-five minutes long) video document of a June 1988 show at London's Dominion Theater, shot by John Maybury. The song selection is pretty much what one would expect from seeing her live, since her set lists did not vary much: **The Value of Ignorance** presents seven songs from **The Lion and the Cobra** and an a cappella encore of a recontextualized Frank O'Connor (no relation) poem "I Am Stretched on Your Grave." Although the product takes its name from the visceral unreleased tune Sinéad was performing at the time, that song does not appear here. The song remains unreleased, except on bootleg cassettes.

Almost the entire **Value of Ignorance** tape is composed of close-up shots of Sinéad. But the shooting style is so intentionally fuzzy that the tight close-ups don't add up to any intimacy with the singer. There is little visual evidence that a band is backing her; the camera rarely pulls back far enough to reveal that. Her accompaniment might as well be in a sound truck across the street. And the audience, also unseen and almost entirely unheard, might as well not have shown up at all.

The Value of Ignorance is as insular as a live recording can be; the tape works like an extended conceptual video that just happened to be recorded onstage. None of what is great about Sinéad works its way onto the tape. What does come through is arty indifference. Sinéad performs some wonderful songs but she does not bother to put them across to anyone but herself. In the end, **The Value of Ignorance** seems like nothing so much as a vanity project and a souvenir for diehard fans. Both Sinéad and her loyal audience deserve better.

One new song from the period that made its way into release was "Jump in the River," which showed up on the soundtrack to Jonathan Demme's warm comedy **Married to the Mob**. Cowritten with Marco Pirroni, it is an immediate leap in songwriting quality from all but the cream of **The Lion and the Cobra**. Sinéad plays nearly all the instruments on the tune (ex-Smiths bassist Andy Rourke pitches in a bass and an acoustic guitar), and she sounds more in control than in any of her previous recordings. The sound of the track is brutal rock (it kicks off with a gun shot), over which Sinéad's wistful tale of a jolting, accidental affair perilously cascades. Not a song so much as it is a resilient riff, "Jump in the River" charges harder than anything on **The Lion and the Cobra**, including "Mandinka," both musically and lyrically. Sinéad's drum-machine pattern is grunge worthy of the Velvet Underground circa **White Light/White Heat**, and her remembrance of hard sex ("There's been days like this before, you know/And I liked it all/Like the times we did it so hard/There was blood on the wall") is potent and vivid.

But "Jump in the River" is about more than an unforgettable interlude; it is about total surrender. The chorus of the song goes "And if you said 'Jump in the river,' I would/Because it would probably be a good idea." Not only does the narrator give in to her lover sexually, she also gives in spiritually. The song is about trust, about giving one's self over to another, and the peace of such a gesture is countered by Sinéad's mammoth electric guitar chords. "Jump in the River" is warm and wild at the same time.

John Maybury's video for the track moves quickly, has dozens of sharp, appropriate on-the-snare-beat cuts, but makes the song sound less decisive than it is. For much of the clip, Sinéad sits at a desk and looks as if she is in some sort of cosmic quandary. The video for "Jump in the River" undermines the song. How can Sinéad's audience get excited about a track if it looks as though she is bored by the whole thing? Not surprisingly, in spite of its great strengths, "Jump in the River" was not much of a hit.

As with "I Want Your (Hands on Me)," Sinéad sought to redefine "Jump in the River" when it came time to remix the inevitable extended version for dance clubs. These remixes got Sinéad across to the hip-hop audience she wanted, but they are also unfair to a performer whose strengths lie elsewhere. The very act of remixing suggests that the performer did not get the song down right the first time it was recorded, but in every case Sinéad's original, self-produced version is preferable to the remix by someone else. Nobody understands her songs better than she does.

Another similarity to "I Want Your (Hands on Me)" lies in the fact that Sinéad pulled in a ringer to help her do the job, in this case controversial performance artist Karen Finley, whom Sinéad had met at a New York benefit for

Refuse and Resist in late 1988. Finley's over-the-top performances were the flip side of Sinéad's more mannered
onstage declamations, and she was a natural counterbal-
ance. As she did with M. C. Lyte, Sinéad brought in Finley
to supply a sound and a tone she could not. And at a time
when censorship forces in the United States were starting
to pick up steam, it was a great slap in their collective
face.

Finley's off-kilter rap in the extended "Jump in the
River" is alternately menacing and crazed by lust, always
built around anatomical descriptions that are considered
obscenities. This was no surprise—Finley's shows have
been known to feature her stuffing a yam into her behind—
but it made explicit the longing implicit in the original
version's tale of life-altering infatuation. In some ways,
Finley's screaming and demands for sex would also have
made sense on the remix of "I Want Your (Hands on
Me)." By evidence of these two dance remixes, Sinéad
perceived these exercises as opportunities for her to pull
into the songs elements of which she was not herself
capable, with a verbal directness that eluded her. Sinéad
was beginning to turn into a classic rock-star control
freak, but she knew her limitations.

So Sinéad was more assured artistically and personally
when she tied the knot with Reynolds. She had more of a
sense of herself and what she could and could not do, and
the chance to be at home with Jake for an extended
period of time gave her even more strength. She was not a
kid anymore, and she was ready to take her life back. She
kept a low profile and tried to settle back into some sort
of normal life. The year on the road had left her chronically
fatigued, and she turned to yoga as a way out.

Sinéad also did one other necessary thing, which was

probably the hardest of all: she fired her manager and her best friend.

Many who have had to deal with Fachtna O'Ceallaigh put him down at the slightest provocation. They say he is too abrasive, he is too opinionated, and he is too anxious to escalate a minor disagreement into thermonuclear war. Still, virtually everyone who dealt with him during the three years he managed Sinéad agree on one thing: O'Ceallaigh did what he thought was best for Sinéad, even if it was not really in her interest.

But instead of helping an artist keep control, which is what a good rock-and-roll manager is supposed to do, O'Ceallaigh controlled Sinéad. Granted, she was a willing subordinate in that she was infatuated enough with O'Ceallaigh and his ideas to go along with anything he said (on the musical side, it is not unfair to suggest that this situation helped inspire "Jump in the River"). No twenty-one-year-old rock star wants to—or should have to—deal with the business side of rock and roll; she wants to lead the charmed life of an artist, where everyone tells her she is a genius and everyone caters to her needs because she is generating the money that pays everyone's salaries. It has become standard to blame everything Sinéad did from 1987 to 1989 on O'Ceallaigh (Sinéad herself does it in interviews when someone brings up O'Ceallaigh), but it is worth remembering that Sinéad was no dope during that time of her life, just a kid. Nobody forced her to sign with O'Ceallaigh, nobody forced her to stay with O'Ceallaigh, nobody forced her to regularly defend O'Ceallaigh.

But by late 1989, Sinéad had outgrown O'Ceallaigh. She wanted complete power over her life and her career, and he was living vicariously through her. Regarding her outbursts on U2 and the Irish Republican Army, it had gotten to the point at which the artist was a mouthpiece for the manager, instead of the other way around. As veteran rock manager Noel Monk points out, once a manager thinks he is the rock star big trouble is inevitable. If Sinéad wanted to grow, O'Ceallaigh—and his clique—had to go. They had gotten too close, and he was holding her back in too many ways. Just as Sinéad had quickly outgrown the ideas of producer Mick Glossop, she had finally outgrown her protector, Fachtna O'Ceallaigh.

O'Ceallaigh's subsequent comments nearly a year later indicated that he still did not understand why he had been sacked. He told **Rolling Stone**'s Mikal Gilmore, ''I never thought of Sinéad as a person or object who made records. I thought of her as a human being and friend.'' In other words, O'Ceallaigh had gotten too close to the person to effectively manage her career without first considering his own feelings. And that spells doom.

Sinéad responded to the breakup like a good artist should: she burrowed into her music and began writing and recording as quickly and as furiously as she could. She huddled in a small studio with engineer Chris Birkett—again, Sinéad intended to produce herself—and sparingly brought other players (Reynolds, Pirroni, Rourke) into the fold, and poured her heart into her new songs. These extremely personal tunes—far more direct and considered than those on **The Lion and the Cobra**—probably would not garner much more of a mass audience, she thought, but it was the most emotionally honest record she could make and that was what was most important.

By year's end, Sinéad found a new manager (Steve Fargnoli, a former member of Prince's management team) and had gone a long way toward repairing her relationship with Ensign's Grainge and Hill, who had heard an early version of the new record and encouraged her to follow her muse, although they were taken aback by its intimacy. They all thought that **I Do Not Want What I Haven't Got** was a great record, but nobody thought it would sell much. It would solidify Sinéad's position as a cult icon, but that was all.

7

I Do Not Want
What I Haven't Got

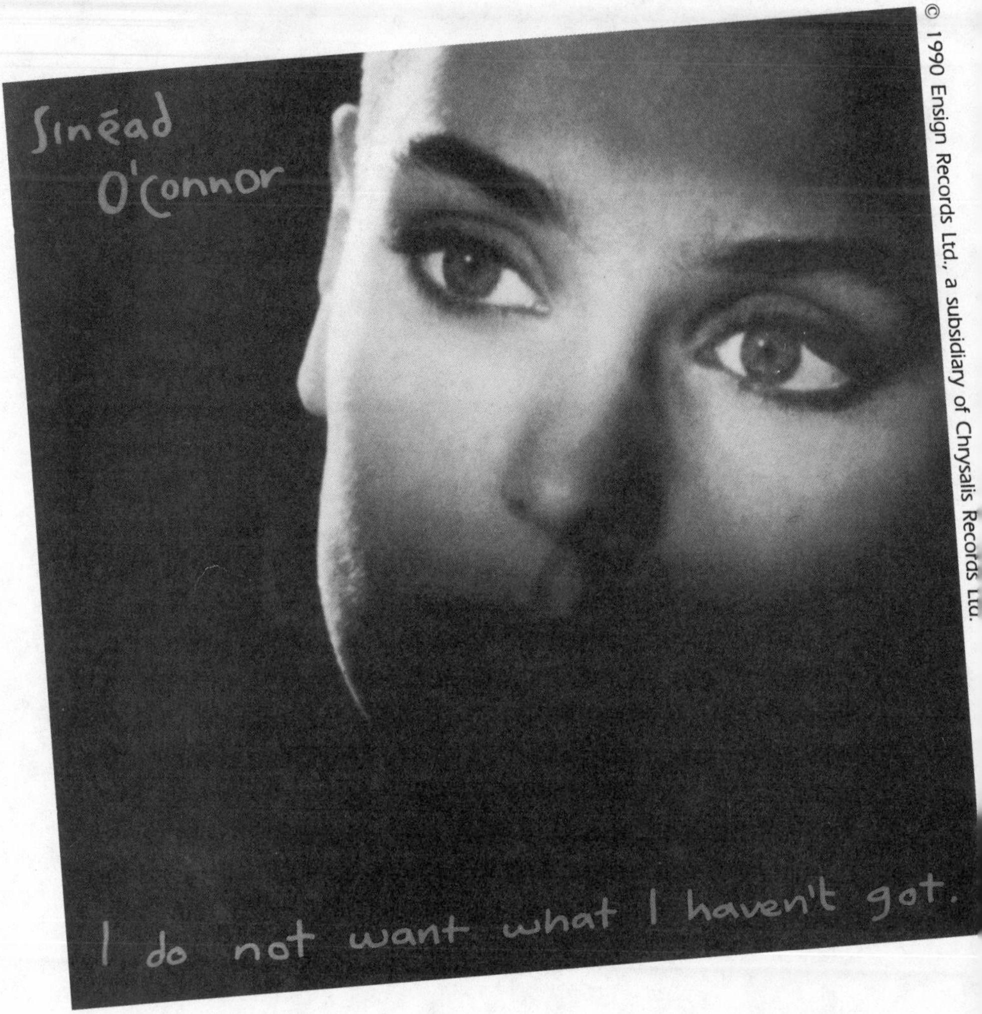
Sinéad
O'Connor
I do not want what I haven't got.

*A*lthough it is great art, Sinéad's second album, **I Do Not Want What I Haven't Got**, was intended to be a record about stripping away artifice. Like John Lennon's myth-shattering **Plastic Ono Band** LP that he made after the Beatles imploded and his dreams fell apart, Sinéad's second album is all about honesty in the face of unremitting, unexplained treachery. **Plastic Ono Band** is a clear precedent even if Sinéad had not heard that unflinching record. On **I Do Not Want What I Haven't Got** Sinéad takes it inside for real, dumps the element of artiness that prevented **The Lion and the Cobra** from living up to its potential, and finds far more that is applicable to the outside world. By going inside, Sinéad's work becomes more open. Instead of going for myth, she discovers that the most personal emotions can yield the most universal songs.

    I Do Not Want What I Haven't Got shows tremendous growth on her part; still, Sinéad remains as ahistorical as pre–**Joshua Tree** U2. The intensity of the album may be of a piece with **Plastic Ono Band** and Van Morrison's **St. Dominic's Preview**, but musically **I Do Not Want What I Haven't Got** bears little relation to either of those landmark albums or to what was happening in pop music in 1990. Its intentionally insular, folk-tinged ballads ran against the beat-imperative zeitgeist. Sinéad may have gone on about how her favorite music was the hard-core rap of Public Enemy's **Fear of a Black Planet** and N.W.A.'s **Straight Outta Compton**, but except for one sampled drum track, **I Do Not Want What I Haven't Got** had nothing in common with rap—unless one counted Sinéad's strong predisposition, maybe even love, for wringing new meaning out of familiar words and phrases. **I Do Not Want What I Haven't Got** is as direct as all but the most brutal rap, but sonically it bears no relation.

What makes **I Do Not Want What I Haven't Got** so moving, for the most part, is Sinéad's ability to plunder the same ideas she first addressed on **The Lion and the Cobra**—betrayal, spirituality, betrayal, unrequited love, and more betrayal—with more assurance and without her debut album's occasional inscrutability. Her musical and lyrical language is much less adorned (i.e., less wordy), and that extra space in her sound and her words gave her freedom and confidence.

Freedom and confidence spark "Feel So Different," the first and longest of the album's ten tracks, clocking in at just under seven minutes. It starts with the Alcoholics Anonymous–derived Serenity Prayer and for a moment the first-time listener worries that he or she has stumbled into a psychotherapy session by accident, that this is going to be a Carly Simon record produced by Shirley MacLaine.

The Serenity Prayer's origins in A.A. aside, it has become an essential invocation of 1980s and 1990s self-help groups, which are supposed to battle codependency and a variety of other personal and societal ills invented by authors of self-help books. This may sound cynical, but it is important to remember that codependency has become a multimillion-dollar industry. New Age cults have become easy ways for entrepreneurs to make quick money and for legions of hurting people to think that they are transcending their problems and failings. Even if these people are helped— and, to be fair, many are—they are still being exploited. Outside of the recording studio, Sinéad and her karma have flirted with Eastern and Middle Eastern belief systems; in addition to yoga, she revealed in **Pulse!**, around the time **I Do Not Want What I Haven't Got** came out, that she has an affinity for numerology, kabbalism (mystical Judaic readings), reincarnation, and daily chanting. She is searching in her music; she is searching in her life.

Fortunately, such New Age fuzziness does not manifest itself in "Feel So Different" after the agenda-setting Serenity Prayer is out of the way. Accompanied by Nick Ingram's sweeping string arrangements, a focused Sinéad begins to sing as if she is indeed a different woman from the one who wrote, performed, and toured behind **The Lion and the Cobra**. She does not sound distracted from trying to squeeze too much into each verse, she does not substitute vocal range for emotional range, and she does not overstate her case. The point of the song's lyrics is that she is a different person, and Sinéad's performance lives up to her words. At first listen, even a fan of the debut album can immediately sense lyrical and musical growth in this manifesto.

Lyrically, "Feel So Different" showcases Sinéad's improved control at addressing lyrics to an imagined second person, an old folkie trick that Bob Dylan turned into a rock-lyric imperative. Those looking for autobiographical references to her break with O'Ceallaigh will find them if they want ("I started off with many friends...I thought they meant every word they said/But like everyone else they were stalling"), yet the breakthrough the lyrics expressed is not so concentrated. She feels different because of a change within herself, not in others.

Next up on **I Do Not Want What I Haven't Got** is "I Am Stretched on Your Grave," the definitive James Brown beat atop a Phillip King melody of a Frank O'Connor poem. The Godfather of Soul never could have foreseen this inspired poem-melody-beat cross-pollination, which deftly accomplishes the failed first-album traditional-contemporary mix, and as a welcome plus listeners do not have to contend with Enya this time. The addition of the sampled Clyde Stubblefield drum track makes the earlier a cappella version of the song from **The Value of Ignorance** sound even more incomplete than before. One of the two great brave remakes on **I Do Not Want What I Haven't Got**, "I Am Stretched on Your Grave" lets Sinéad fantasize for five and one-half minutes about being the world's first Gaelic rapper. Steve Wickham's circular fiddle on the coda completes the circle. The track works well coming right after "Feel So Different" by showing how Sinéad's new-found strength is the vehicle by which she has become able to dig deeper into her Irish heritage and link it with her more newfound love, rap music and hip-hop culture.

The music on "Three Babies" bears a superficial similarity to that of "Feel So Different," with its Ingram-directed strings and Sinéad's breathless delivery, but here the spiritual aspects are more neatly integrated into both the song proper and its performance. The song's devotional aspects serve as its hook: Sinéad reverently shivers through a tale of surrender even less equivocal than the one that pro-

In ''Troy,'' Sinéad sang she'd kill a dragon. She never said anything about cleaning up afterward. (LONDON FEATURES INTERNATIONAL)

Sinéad performs ''Mandinka'' at the 1988 Grammy Awards. (AP/ WIDE WORLD PHOTOS)

Dancing with abandon on the first leg of the 1990 tour. Her necklace suggests that "Nothing Compares 2 U" isn't all she swiped from Prince. (PAUL ROBICHEAU)

The reluctant pop star poses at a 1988 press conference.
(Paul Robicheau)

(PAUL ROBICHEAU)

No, she's not doing a Stevie Nicks impersonation. (Paul Robicheau)

Bopping to "The Emperor's New Clothes": "How could I possibly know what I want / when I'm only twenty-three?" (PAUL ROBICHEAU)

(PAUL ROBICHEAU)

Is that a wig under the cap? (LONDON FEATURES INTERNATIONAL)

Onstage in Berlin. (JANA/STAR FILE)

Acting out "I Want Your (Hands on Me)." Rapper M. C. Lyte is nowhere to be found. (PAUL ROBICHEAU)

Shouting out "Mandinka" on the *Lion and the Cobra* tour.
(Paul Robicheau)

Sinéad's first American performance, at the World in New York City. Note the button. (NICK ELGAR/LFI)

The end of a bad day (look under her left eye). (GEOFF SWAINE/LFI)

Burrowing deeply into the song... (NICK ELGAR/LFI)

Sinéad with Van Morrison, her greatest musical influence, at Roger Waters's *The Wall* concert in Berlin. (Rex Features/RDR Productions)

pelled "Jump in the River." She had found something that "proved things I never believed," and the joy of the performance sounds hard-fought: she sang of blaspheming and denial. Sinéad sings along with her lanky acoustic guitar chords and august synthesizer lines (except for the strings, she is the only musician on the number), thrilled by the words she recites. The three babies of the title could be a variety of people. Some have suggested that they are the singer, her husband, and their son; others have hypothesized that they are the Holy Trinity. Whoever these elevated babies are, they inspired Sinéad to write a moving song of praise. This is a blissful, grand imagining, but it still has an edge.

"The Emperor's New Clothes" has a dumb title conceit; otherwise it is a perfect pop song. The first straight-ahead rock tune on **I Do Not Want What I Haven't Got**, it is an ideal example of lyrical imagination presented as autobiography. The narrator is a woman in the public eye with a young child, which sounds more than a little like Sinéad herself, as it is supposed to. But when listeners reduce the song to straight autobiography, it diminishes the deftness, resourcefulness, and professionalism of Sinéad's songwriting.

Many artists want their work to reflect real life, but true-to-life art does not have to be a documentary. It is like when Carly Simon surprised everyone by putting out a good song, "You're So Vain," and instead of reveling in the song itself, most people seemed more interested in figuring out if the song was addressed to Warren Beatty. (Some people never learn; nowadays rock critics wonder the same thing about Madonna songs.) Because Sinéad frequently declares that her songs are extremely personal, she opens the door to such interpretations. But in doing so she sells herself short and invites her fans and critics to do the same. She is an artist; she is not a journal writer.

Here is a quick example of why taking such a song 100 percent literally is inherently stupid. In the first verse of "The Emperor's New Clothes," Sinéad claims, "And there's millions of people/To offer advice and say how I should be/But they're twisted/And they will never be any influence on me." A literal reading of those lines would suggest that Sinéad had an active audience in the millions (not true when she wrote the song) and that she thinks the members of that active audience are foolish (probably not true). This would be in keeping with the knee-jerk critics who accused Dire Straits' Mark Knopfler of being a racist and a homophobe because the narrator of one of his songs, "Money for Nothing," had those ugly ideas. The narrator of the song was also an appliance delivery man, but no one accused him of being that. Randy Newman, who writes regularly of racists, rapists, and dumb rock stars, frequently receives similar criticism.

Pervasive sentiments across a career are one thing, but one song is not a career. Writers are allowed to create characters, though many writers, including rock lyricists, are incapable of inventing characters who do not have a great deal in common with their originators. Until Sinéad titles a song or a record **The Story of My Life**, listeners should not use her songs as an excuse to say they know something about her private life.

Part of what makes "The Emperor's New Clothes" sublime is that it takes autobiography as its starting point and then, thanks to its supple chords, leaps in a dozen fertile directions. (Randy Newman pulled off the same trick on the first few tracks of his **Land of Dreams** record.) "The Emperor's New Clothes" does so much. It inverts the Dylan method of putting down an imagined second person used in "Feel So Different" by making that imagined second person alternately loved and detested. It celebrates domesticity and at the same time it announces the outgrowing of a sponsor—perhaps O'Ceallaigh? It is alternately self-righteous and accommodating: it reveals in its own acknowledgedly self-contradictory message. Like "Mandinka," another song on which guitarist Pirroni was a substantial presence, "The Emperor's New Clothes" unrolls an exemplary mix of acoustic and electric guitars. Sinéad's acoustic lines caress Pirroni's more aggressive electric ones, reinforcing the similar relationship in the lyrics.

"The Emperor's New Clothes" goes out on a powerful, willfully repetitious outro in which the band keeps steady and plays the chords harder and harder. The rocking outro lasts ninety seconds, less on the hacked single version, but it never bores; this quartet could play these chords all night if they wanted to and there was enough tape.

Unfortunately, the song's only forced element comes right before that wise outro. The title of the song does not appear in the lyrics until Sinéad repeats it four times and dances into the outro. Because the title is a cliché—and a cliché with no resonance, at that—it does not resolve the song as well as it should. Sinéad thought hard about every other element in "The Emperor's New Clothes"; the song deserves a better idea to hold it together. Still, the giddy enthusiasm of the music and the angular irony of "The Emperor's New Clothes" is enough to make it an instant classic.

In the fall of 1990, Chrysalis released a remix of "The Emperor's New Clothes" with the original rhythm track erased and a new, inappropriate one, aimed at dancers looking for house music, grafted on. Its complete failure underlines how deeply the words and music of the original worked together; they were inextricable and the loss of one made the other sound empty.

Quieter than "The Emperor's New Clothes" but even more intense is "Black Boys on Mopeds," which Sinéad plays alone, accompanied only by her Takamine twelve-string acoustic guitar and an overdubbed harmony. Arranged by Sinéad with World Party's Karl Wallinger, who had developed into an ace pop dissector, "Black Boys on Mopeds" is a protest song whose beauty enhances the ugly tale it tells.

"Black Boys on Mopeds" is about the inarguable disintegration of Great Britain under its prime minister of more than a decade, Margaret Thatcher, the Tories' Iron Lady. The song's images are despairing and bold, and it takes its title conceit from the pointless death of Nicholas Bramble, a young man on a moped pursued by policemen who thought he had stolen it. Terrified, Bramble sped up and was killed when his bike crashed; the consensus was that Bramble would not have been scrutinized had he not been a black man. Although an inquiry absolved the police of wrongdoing and the accident was technically caused by Bramble's own mistake, Bramble's was a death that would have been inconceivable without the malevolent intervention of the authorities, and it is emotionally right—if not legally right—for Sinéad to charge England as "the home of police/Who kill black boys on mopeds."

"Black Boys on Mopeds" is the shortest song on **I Do Not Want What I Haven't Got**, but in many ways it covers the most ground. It is full of exaggerations that appalled many, but all political art is founded upon exaggeration. Again, that is the difference between creative art and documentary art. The exaggeration that turned off the most people was its first verse, in which the narrator is puzzled that Thatcher was "shocked" by the Chinese government's brutal attack on its own people in Beijing's Tiananmen Square, because "the same orders are given by her." Sure, the bloodthirst of Thatcher manifests itself less blatantly than that of Li Peng, but the exaggeration sounds like one necessitated because no one listens to the plain truth. Thatcher allowed a war to happen in the South Atlantic, fought over sheep and pride, that left many dead for no good reason. And if she considers the rule of the Li Peng regime morally and politically bankrupt, why is she allowing the British to maintain power by force in Ireland? In "Black Boys on Mopeds," emotions make more sense than facts.

Once again, it is impossible for even a fan of **The Lion and the Cobra** to listen to this track from **I Do Not Want What I Haven't Got** without being amazed at the tremendous growth of every element of Sinéad's art. Comparing this deep performance with the affectations of her debut is unfair; suffice it to say that, to paraphrase the most-quoted line in "The Emperor's New Clothes," how could she have possibly known what she wanted when she was only twenty-one? Two years later, she is still young, but she is much more thoughtful as a writer, performer, and producer.

The slender acoustic guitar lines frame "Black Boys on Mopeds," and Sinéad's voice jumps to make points. The song is addressed to someone older than she, a former idealist who has grown cold, and Sinéad is both loving and emphatic in her response to the person who used to be what she is now. In the last verse, Sinéad makes her case for separation from worldly things, an idea that also pops up in "The Emperor's New Clothes" ("I see plenty of clothes that I like/But I won't go anywhere nice for a while") and is made explicit in the anti-yuppie, antimaterialistic title track. In Sinéad's view of the world, there is sacred and there is profane; like the work of Prince circa **Sign o' the Times**, **The Black Album**, and **Lovesexy**, Sinéad's work examines the pull of both sides but in the end comes down squarely on one side. She wants to be Good.

Prince furnished **I Do Not Want What I Haven't Got**

with its most revelatory ballad, in Sinéad's hands the most all-encompassing song of unrequited love since "Layla" by Derek and the Dominoes: "Nothing Compares 2 U." Sinéad was introduced to this song by O'Ceallaigh, and her performance goes so far beyond commitment it is sometimes difficult to believe she did not write it.

Prince wrote "Nothing Compares 2 U" for the Family, one of his lesser protégé groups. The Family was born out of Prince's desire to give work to the few members of the Time who did not desert him after **Purple Rain** hit, and also to provide a vehicle for Susannah Melvoin (twin sister of Wendy Melvoin, then the guitarist in Prince's band, the Revolution), who may or may not have been his lover. (Tracking Prince's liaisons is far more treacherous and tiring than shadowing Sinéad's.) The group's one album was a cluttered mess that straddled the border between the most pop-oriented elements of psychedelia and the most pop-oriented elements of funk. But as the Firesign Theater once asked, how can you be in two places at once when you are not anywhere at all? The Family's sole single was "Screams of Passion," in which Melvoin ostensibly faked an orgasm for the microphone—an idea that seemed idiotic a decade earlier when Donna Summer and Andrea True did it and now sounded idiotic and dated. Melvoin was not believable; rather than climaxing, she sounded like she was just about to sneeze. If she had landed a job on a phone-sex line, Melvoin would have been fired on her first day.

In the hands of the Family, "Nothing Compares 2 U" was merely Prince's latest codependency-anthem ballad, with unexpected chord changes that verged on the Baroque, and were of a piece with the lesser of Prince's other **Parade/Under the Cherry Moon**—era ballads. The orchestration is overblown, wooden, an utterly unbelievable exercise. Anyone who wonders why nobody wanted the Family to record a second album only has to listen to this. Many who have heard Sinéad's version of "Nothing Compares 2 U" have responded to it immediately; one's respect for her performance should be that much greater for pulling that song out of its horrible origins and making it the hardest easy-listening number one record in years, a version even Prince himself has applauded.

Sinéad coproduced her take of "Nothing Compares 2 U" with the person who at the time was the latest attempt by England to produce its own Prince, Nellee Hooper of the funk unit Soul II Soul. Hooper's version of funk is far more constricted than Prince's, but he turned out to be an appropriate collaborator with Sinéad on this cut.

"Nothing Compares 2 U" opens sparsely, just a synthesizer. "It's been seven hours and fifteen days/Since U took your love away," Sinéad warbles, wandering into the song. Something is amiss. Sinéad's singing is as technically astounding as it always is, but there is a catch in her tenor, something holding her back. Midway through the verse, drums crash in and maintain the painful, slow pace, but it is not offering the singer any relief. Sinéad plows forward, devastated, aware only of her own pain.

The song stays spare; the singer and her overwhelming sadness are always up front. She has absolute freedom but cannot live without her lover. Her doctor is no help. All the flowers in her backyard have died. She knows "that living with you, baby, was sometimes hard/But I'm willing to give it another try/'Cos nothing compares...2 U." The language of heartbreak here is as unflinching as the singer wants to sound unsure. Still, she is willing to fight for her lover.

This leads to the fundamental contradiction of "Nothing

Compares 2 U" and the main element it shares in common with "Layla." In Sinéad's hands, "Nothing Compares 2 U" is as bereft of hope as Hank Williams's "Lost Highway" or Robert Johnson's "Love in Vain," but she sings it with such phenomenal lung power that it is impossible to conceive of her as someone as drained as she claims to be. If she can sing this hard, this intently, she was probably too good for whoever left her. She is a strong woman, one who will persevere. She is strong. Forget her lover: nothing compares to her.

"Jump in the River," the **Married to the Mob** soundtrack cut of the previous year, is the next number, and it peeks in on the same relationship at least sixteen days earlier. Sinéad's rough guitar riff never develops into a full song, but this hard-yet-submissive tune succeeds on insouciance alone. It works well on **I Do Not Want What I Haven't Got** following the desolation of "Nothing Compares 2 U," providing both lyrical and rhythmic relief.

Such relief is short-lived, because the next two songs are anguished originals. "You Cause as Much Sorrow" is a sweet but intense put-down, as the singer herself acknowledges: "It just sounds more vicious/Than I actually mean/I really am soft and tender and sweet." As intimate as "Three Babies" and "Black Boys on Mopeds," the bitterness of "You Cause as Much Sorrow" is cloaked in half-whispered vocals, until Sinéad rises to deliver the gallows-humor title punch line: "You cause as much sorrow dead/As you did when you were alive." This is codependency at its most insidious, although Sinéad's incessant exploration in her songs of her childhood beliefs will lead some to believe that she is addressing this song to Jesus Christ. In recent interviews Sinéad has talked disparagingly of organized religion, but at the same time she makes clear that she is extremely familiar with the Catholic Church.

Sinéad has never been shy about calling the Church on the issues that she feels gnawed at her parents' failed marriage and at her. Around the time she was writing the songs for **I Do Not Want What I Haven't Got**, Sinéad made her acting debut in **Hush-a-Bye Baby**, a film that was part of the Dublin Film Festival and appeared on British television. Sinéad's role was that of a fifteen-year-old girl (with hair; she wore a wig) whose friend becomes pregnant. "It just shows some of the bad effects an Irish Catholic upbringing can have on young girls," Sinéad told **Pulse!** of the film, which had as its factual basis the story of Anne Lovett, an Irish girl found dead at a grotto for the Madonna, clutching her dead baby. The **I Do Not Want What I Haven't Got** track "Three Babies" was originally written for **Hush-a-Bye Baby**, which leads to yet another possible interpretation as to who the narrator is supposed to be, especially considering the line "I have wrapped your cold bodies around me."

"Why can't you just let me be?" Sinéad asks in "You Cause as Much Sorrow" beside piano swells, with the exasperation of someone who has asked the question a thousand times before, suggesting no one so much as Hazel Motes, the Jesus-pursued hero of Flannery O'Connor's Church-dogmatic novel **Wise Blood**. Although Sinéad is probably unfamiliar with the work of this antecedent, Flannery O'Connor was a fellow Irish Catholic obsessed with the evil of worldliness and the need to stand away from it. Sinéad picks up the baton a generation after Flannery's premature death, although Sinéad writes from experience, not a bedroom on her mother's farm. Flannery was an observer and came down resolutely on the side of grace; Sinéad is a participant and her morality plays are closer to a lived life. Sinéad accepts some Catholic dogma—she has said in interviews that she believes in an afterlife—but she reserves the right to a line-item veto of each element of the faith.

Yet the next song is so grounded in the narrator's experience that Sinéad does not bother pondering whether the story has two sides. "The Last Day of Our Acquaintance" is the most pitiless song on **I Do Not Want What I Haven't Got**; it is the most honest, unsparing song about a break-up since Sam Phillips's "Out of Time" (from her **The Indescribable Wow!** collection), and Phillips's song is far more generous. In "The Last Day of Our Acquaintance," it is clear from the performance if not the lyrics that the narrator has been the slighted one. The arrangement, based around Reynolds's titanic drums, sets off quiet explosions as Sinéad puts down a soon-to-be-ex-spouse as she fantasizes a divorce meeting in a lawyer's office at which "I'll talk but you won't listen to me." The listener never does find out what tore them apart, but it is clear that the narrator holds herself blameless. By the end of the song the band is screaming for more and more room: Reynolds demolishes everything in his path, and bassist Jah Wobble caresses the beat without softening it. (Wobble, long-ago bassist for John Lydon's post–Sex Pistols band Public Image Limited, was considered even more anachronistic than Pirroni, but here he shines.) The rhythm section recalls no one so much as Crazy Horse.

"Two years ago the seed was planted," Sinéad yells, apparently referring to a surprise pregnancy. Around the time **I Do Not Want What I Haven't Got** came out, Sinéad told **Time** that her goal was to "write harshly." Here is a song harsher than any of her interviews in support of **The Lion and the Cobra**, and this time no one is putting words into her mouth. The anger is hers, and she is a woman of action.

After the explosion of "The Last Day of Our Acquaintance" comes the magical fallout of "I Do Not Want What I Haven't Got." It is a closely microphoned a cappella track that opens with a big breath and over six ravishing minutes retraces a path no less malevolent than the one in **Pilgrim's Progress**. Sinéad walks through the Valley of the Shadow, and emerges wiser and more serene. She holds notes as long as she can, so in love with the tale that she cannot let go. Not before or since has her singing ever sounded so at peace, so untroubled.

"I Do Not Want What I Haven't Got" is the album's culminating manifesto. Its tale of a spiritual search picks up where the lead-off number "Feel So Different" ended and comments on the intervening eight cuts, which upon reflection detail precisely the sorts of spiritual challenges she alludes to in the title track. Recorded in the last days of one of the greediest decades through which Western civilization has suffered, a pop star says Enough Already. Sinéad has the luxury to sing "I have all that I requested/ And I do not want what I haven't got." She has suffered trials, she has survived them, and all she wants to do is lead a quiet, normal life.

The only problem was that as soon as people heard the album **I Do Not Want What I Haven't Got**, it was clear that never again would Sinéad be able to lead such a life. Ironically, her statement of financial and spiritual contentment would make her a millionaire.

8

Superstar

S ome executives at Ensign and Chrysalis, none of whom will admit it now, were worried that **I Do Not Want What I Haven't Got** was too personal to become a massive hit, but they were also aware that they had underestimated the commercial potential of **The Lion and the Cobra** by a factor of twenty. Advance sales were encouraging, and they crossed their fingers. Ego aside, they wanted to be wrong about this. It had not been a great year for the label; they needed a hit.

Still, they were worried, and they had the example of Terence Trent D'Arby fresh in their minds to worry them even more. D'Arby's debut album, **Introducing the Hardline According to Terence Trent D'Arby**, had been a bracing dissection of a variety of soul and pop styles that sold two million copies while D'Arby provided copy almost as inflammatory as Sinéad's. Live he covered performers as diverse as the Rolling Stones and Sam Cooke, and he cut them both: he was that good. But D'Arby's follow-up, **Neither Fish nor Flesh**, was not what people expected and it bombed. Instead of soul alone being the base this time, **Neither Fish nor Flesh** sprang from a broader mix of sweet soul, swamp rock, psychedelia, and Prince. D'Arby's second album was wild, it was weird, and even though it was frequently visionary nobody in the industry could figure out what to do with it. (Elvis Costello had released a similarly diverse collection, **Spike**, around the same time, but he got away with it because he was white. African-American performers who do not conform to expectations, who are considered "experimental" by a rock industry that stops listening after ten seconds if it thinks the record in question is not a hit, do not have a chance.) The lyrics of **Neither Fish nor Flesh** were personal and perceived as obtuse (though no more obtuse than, say, platinum art-rockers Rush), and D'Arby's new attitude— just as assured but far less over the top—was not nearly as effective a selling tack. Chrysalis executives bit what remained of their nails.

What was worse about the commercial failure of **Neither Fish nor Flesh**—other than that it denied a worthy performer a chance to grow and learn in public—was the inevitable chilling effect it had on other second albums by artists who wanted to be adventurous. Using **Neither Fish nor Flesh** as an example, tremendous pressure was exerted on many performers who had scored big the first time out not to change a good thing. Many performers acquiesced. A variety of second albums released in 1990—from the Jeff Healy Band to the Indigo Girls—were markedly less interesting than their predecessors, to a great extent because they replowed fields that had been adequately picked the first time around.

Record companies got so scared, so cynical, and so greedy at the time that they would not even bother to commission or finance the recording of new material for a performer's second album: Virgin followed up Paula Abdul's megaplatinum debut **Forever Your Girl** with **Shut Up and Dance**, remixes of seven songs from the debut; Arista followed up Milli Vanilli's even-more megaplatinum debut **Girl You Know It's True** with the similar **The Remix Album**. The new releases were, as expected, safe, boring, and successful, enough so to make rock fans fear that this would become a pervasive practice. Abdul and Milli Vanilli were not producing great art the first time out; listening to their second albums was like watching reruns of "Who's the Boss?"

The same problem that afflicted D'Arby's sales could zoom in on Abdul and Milli Vanilli the next time around. Although the formulaic nature of both performers' work makes that an unlikely prospect, it is possible. But if it does happen and these performers do fall out of commercial favor, it will have been on their third album, not their second, and their record companies will have already made a lot more money. Perhaps Paula Abdul and Milli Vanilli will keep rereleasing the same album for the next decade, with titles like **The Original Demos, Having Fun Lip-Synching on Stage, The Video Mixes**, and **Greatest Hits (So Far)**. By that time, their labels could compile the obligatory multi-CD box sets. The album title **Forever Your Girl** never seemed so ominous.

That scenario is exaggeration (at least one hopes it is), but it indicates how intensely record-company officials want their sophomore performers to stick to what worked just fine the first time around. And although clear heads may have recognized that **I Do Not Want What I Haven't Got** was a far more substantial and lasting work of art than **The Lion and the Cobra**, those clear heads also wanted their salaries covered. But such objections were overruled when they saw the video that stalwart John Maybury had directed for "Nothing Compares 2 U."

Aided by an all-female crew, Maybury had shot a moody clip for the Prince cover tune, tracking a forlorn-looking Sinéad as she walked around a park; gargoyles provided color and relief. For the requisite lip-synch shots, Sinéad performed in tight close-up, the camera reaching from her forehead only as far down as the top of her black turtle-neck sweater. Sinéad was unavoidable, all-encompassing; viewers could not look away from the waif.

When it came time to edit the "Nothing Compares 2 U" clip, it instantly became clear to Maybury and Sinéad that the tracking footage was adequate, but the close-up footage was simply amazing. It had to be the basis for the entire clip. Filmed against a black background, the minimalistic, iconoclastic shots were an affront to the excessive videos that clog MTV and other channels. If anything, "Nothing Compare 2 U" is an antivideo, an antidote to MTV. This was as close to direct communica-tion as one could offer in a lip-synch situation: one wom-an, her face filling the screen, devastated, uncloaked. The tear that runs down her cheek toward the end of the song is not stage glycerine; it indicates how deeply Sinéad believes in the song, how deeply she identifies with it, and how deeply it inspires her. Sinéad tries to keep her gaze fixed on the camera, but frequently she has to look away, sometimes toward the floor, sometimes toward the sky.

It is one of these latter, heaven-directed scans that Sinéad decided to use as the album/cassette/compact disc cover for **I Do Not Want What I Haven't Got**. The cover still is a 180-degree turn from the tortured shot that graced **The Lion and the Cobra**. Here, Sinéad looks at peace with herself (it is amazing how different a shot can look out of context), keeping in line with the title of the album and the driving idea behind it. It was also effective cross-marketing, in that those most familiar with the image of Sinéad in the "Nothing Compares 2 U" video could now bring home that image along with the music.

One cannot underestimate the importance of the "Nothing Compares 2 U" video when trying to understand why the single "Nothing Compares 2 U" and the album **I Do Not Want What I Haven't Got** were such massive smash hits so quickly. The video was not merely a refreshing break from the scantily clad models and hairy-chested heavy-metal cretins who usually fill the video wave. "Nothing Compares 2 U" also reintroduces Sinéad as a vulnerable performer to those put off by her Grammy-night aggressiveness, and made a strong impression on those who had never before seen her. Love-song ballads without Tin Pan Alley or heavy-metal starting points are a rarity in rock, so the visual manifestation of even a mediocre ballad of that sort has high hopes. Also, because the clip was mostly tight close-up, her crew cut (she had briefly let her hair grow a bit) did not get the chance to alienate anyone. All in view was a woman singing; each viewer could construct his or her own imagined reality behind it. The video was anything any viewer wanted it to be.

Only a month after the single and video came out, "Nothing Compares 2 U" and **I Do Not Want What I Haven't Got** sat at the top of **Billboard**'s pop singles and album charts. The trade paper credited a substantial increase in record-store sales to traffic caused by the excitement over the new Sinéad LP. Said one retail executive, "Sinéad O'Connor just made things explode." Trans World Music Corp., a chain of 437 stores, reported that **I Do Not Want What I Haven't Got** was the chain's top-selling album from the day it was released. Chrysalis hustled to press as many copies as possible. In the United Kingdom, I

Do Not Want What I Haven't Got topped the album charts in its first week of release: not a rare occurrence in a music industry bent on responding fast to a new trend, but still a notable achievement.

Up in New England, a market that had been kind to Sinéad the first time around, the 125-unit Strawberries chain claimed that the only albums that sold better in their first week out than **I Do Not Want What I Haven't Got** were **The Joshua Tree** and Bruce Springsteen's epic live collection. Both U2 and Springsteen were long-established performers when those records came out—**The Joshua Tree** was U2's fifth full-length album; **Live/1975–1985** was Springsteen's eighth. Both had longtime devoted followings that expanded from cult to the mainstream; Sinéad had no such history behind her—just one good record and a tremendous street reputation—which makes the out-of-the-box achievement that much more startling. Strawberries reported that **I Do Not Want What I Haven't Got** was outselling the chain's second-best-selling title by a phenomenal ratio of five to one. "Nothing Compares 2 U" was the year's first genuine platinum single (other platinum certifications had been given out, but those included twelve-inch-single sales, which are prorated). In one stunning day, **I Do Not Want What I Haven't Got** sold more than half a million albums, or nearly as many albums as **The Lion and the Cobra** did in a full year of release. In a material sense, Sinéad had more than she ever dreamed.

Sinéad's rising fortunes also had an immediate, direct impact on the company that feared that **I Do Not Want What I Haven't Got** was not commercial enough. Chrysalis reported a quarterly profit of $2.3 million against a $3.5 million loss in the same period a year earlier: Sinéad's insular musings had gotten fans back into stores and turned around an entire company. In September 1990, Chrysalis announced that its international gross proceeds had nearly doubled from the previous year.

The success of **I Do Not Want What I Haven't Got** followed the same road Chrysalis traveled to break **The Lion and the Cobra**, but Chrysalis had a running start and, since Sinéad was already a known quantity in some areas, the company's promotion staff started far ahead from where they did the first time out. Instead of starting at college radio, the bottom rung of the radio ladder, building a beachhead there, and moving on to album radio, as they did the first time, Chrysalis started working the natural multiformat smash at album radio and adult-contemporary formats (those easy-listening stations designed to cure insomnia), and then set their sights on top forty CHR (contemporary hits radio) stations. At every level, the video to "Nothing Compares 2 U" was the strongest selling tool of the Chrysalis promotion force. Album radio did not need a hard sell as it did the first time; by the time "Nothing Compares 2 U" had topped the pop charts, many AOR stations had already begun regularly tracking "The Emperor's New Clothes" without any prodding from the Chrysalis staff.

The rock press was also heavily exploited. Reviews were almost universally laudatory (an early notice in **Rolling Stone** quickly got the ball rolling) and Sinéad's interviews read like true confessions. The interviews were explications and expansions of the ideas she had floated in "Feel So Different." Without explicitly denying O'Ceallaigh, Sinéad talked about how appalled she now felt about her comments about the Irish Republican Army, how much she loved her husband and her son, and how she would resolutely not become a typical superstar no matter how big she became. She was repentant for much of her public behavior of the two years past, and she seemed forthright; she sounded like someone becoming comfortable being an adult.

Because Sinéad was now famous, those in the record industry who did not care about music (i.e., too many of them) focused on her shiny scalp and made that the new hook. Columnists in local newspapers made gratuitous remarks about her hair—some labeled her upcoming tour "Bald Ambition," a play on Madonna's "Blonde Ambition" tour name—and in doing so merely revealed how uncomfortable the supposedly liberal American press is about people who are truly different. The first thing ignorant people do with threatening outsiders they do not understand is make fun of them, but that only shows how small-minded many are. Sinéad was an easy target: bald, tiny, and female; the bullies of press and radio wasted no time looking for obvious ways to poke fun at her. **Rolling Stone** ran a cartoon of a bald, dour Sinéad flanked by hair cutouts in the styles of Madonna, Marge Simpson, and other American cultural icons. The cartoon was called "Rock and Roll Makeover: The Do I Want Is the One I've Got." If **Rolling Stone**, a strong supporter of Sinéad, was making fun of her, what would the even more entrenched status quo do?

"I've listened to her album and it's a really serious, artistic piece," acknowledged a producer at WHTZ-FM in New York, one of the country's leading CHR outlets. "But the fact that she has short hair and the fact that she's very unique opens up the joke pile." This is cynicism, which is far less excusable than stupidity.

WHTZ was one of many stations that held contests in which listeners who shaved their head would win something Sinéad-related. (None of those radio geniuses thought to work up a joint promotion with a local hair-replacement franchise.) WMMS-FM in Cleveland had four listeners cut off their hair for a leather jacket and a pair of concert tickets. In Chicago, WKQX-FM disk jockey Robert Murphy put a bounty of five hundred dollars on the toupee of bald rival WBBM-FM disk jockey Joe Bohannon, who in turn lent his twenty toupees to listeners and dared Murphy to come up with the ten thousand dollars. Over the din of this nonsense, it was hard to hear the music. At least at a Sinéad concert what gets in the way of the music are enthusiastic fans; here the problem was self-promoting static.

The rock industry and American media have a rich history of trivializing the work of performers who want to be artists, especially in recent years. For example, when Bruce Springsteen set sales records in 1984 and 1985 with **Born in the U.S.A.**, there were attempts to reduce his dark, questioning tales of a betrayed U.S.A. to fist-pumping **Rambo**-style jingoism (all Springsteen had in common with Sylvester Stallone was his biceps). Jingoistic automobile executive Lee Iacocca tried to get Springsteen to lend his voice to a Chrysler commercial, and when Springsteen told Iacocca what he could do with his 12 million dollars Iacocca got someone else to impersonate Springsteen (Kenny Rogers, of all people). So to undiscerning ears, Iacocca did get Springsteen to do the commercial—no doubt at a fraction of the cost. After Springsteen became a superstar he lost some control. Others were allowed to define his image and his values: both Ronald Reagan and Walter Mondale claimed Springsteen as a supporter during that fact-free election campaign. The ominous undercurrent of Springsteen's music was replaced by the most simpleminded, unquestioning sort of patriotism that the establishment far preferred.

It was precisely this fate that terrified Sinéad as she saw

I Do Not Want What I Haven't Got and "Nothing Compares 2 U" leapfrog up the charts. She was instantly recognizable both visually and musically, and she tried hard to ally herself more closely with the people she knew before she was a famous magazine cover, like the Dublin girl friends she endearingly calls the "beautiful bitches." Sinéad was thrilled and tickled that her music was reaching a much larger audience, but she wanted her life to remain hers.

As she began the first of two lengthy treks across media-hungry America, Sinéad pledged to make an effort to remain normal. She knew it would be hard; she had just separated again from Reynolds.

9

Controversy

*S*inéad began her 1990 American tour as an unlikely new star; she ended it as the most controversial pop performer around at a time when pop performers were causing commotions everywhere.

Sinéad started that tour with a number one record and a lump in her throat. She had left Reynolds once again (he busied himself drumming for the British group Max) at a time when it seemed that every magazine offered an interview in which Sinéad celebrated domestic bliss with Reynolds in the most ebullient terms. With her life in such flux, it must have been difficult reading what seemed like clips from another century (magazines often have lead times of two months or more between delivery of article and publication). Sinéad soon started seeing Hugh Harris, her opening act, a pairing that remained comfortably private until a magazine started paying Jake's nanny for information on the affair. Jake was soon sent back to England.

The early part of the tour was all unencumbered triumph. No one thought to ask her personal questions; the music

and the video did all the talking. Solo appearances on
MTV Unplugged and **VH-1 New Visions** solidified her
position as a changed, major artist, and her first few
performances before sold-out theater audiences were intense,
affirmative affairs greeted with near-Messianic fervor. They
were love-ins without the hippie trappings. During her
show in Boston at the Orpheum, the second date of the
tour, two young girls in the orchestra seats yelled, "We love
you, Sinéad!" between songs—and sometimes during the
quiet songs. Audiences seemed to know the words to all the
songs from **I Do Not Want What I Haven't Got** by heart.
Sinéad was not intimidated by her welcome, but she was
careful not to take advantage of it or become a typical rock
star. This was unlikely no matter how large a hall she filled; it
is impossible to imagine Sinéad shouting, "Good evening
[your city here]! Are you ready to rock and roll?!"

Sinéad's five-piece band was well rehearsed, but not
overrehearsed. Recreating for an audience the songs Sinéad
had imagined for **I Do Not Want What I Haven't Got**,
they supported her adequately but never forgot who
the star was. They rocked out on "Mandinka" and "The
Emperor's New Clothes" and cushioned her during the
ballads. Some nights the highlight was "The Last Day of
Our Acquaintance," which began as the quietest of ballads and ended with everyone raving. As if the tune was
not unwavering enough on record, Sinéad played a longer
version of it live, with an unsparing extra verse: "You were
no life raft to me/I drowned in pain and misery/You did
nothing to stop me/Now drown in your own self-pity."
With this new verse, "The Last Day of Our Acquaintance"
became the greatest rock-and-roll revenge song since "96
Tears" by Question Mark and the Mysterians; Sinéad
played the song with bitter glee.

She learned more about her songs by playing them

every night, and she learned more about herself by adding new songs to her set. One of these tunes was Mary Black's "Anarchie Gordon," another love-meets-death song that makes one understand why Sinéad finds it "comforting" to live near a cemetery back in London. When she spoke of death to **Musician**'s Bill Flanagan, a perceptive interviewer of songwriters, and said that when she dies, "I'm suddenly going to know everything that I don't know now that confuses me or makes me wonder. I'm suddenly going to see it all clearly and it's going to be amazing," one hopes that she was putting Flanagan on, but it seems doubtful. No wonder she wears black so much of the time.

Back in the real world, Sinéad also got herself booked onto the May 12 installment of the formerly innovative comedy-variety series "Saturday Night Life." By 1990 the NBC show had long lost all of the daring and spontaneity that had characterized its first few seasons. In its fifteenth season, "Saturday Night Life" was just a variety show. However, it was a variety show with an audience in the tens of millions, so bands that were offered spots on the show did not turn it down.

Around the same time, "Saturday Night Life" nabbed a host for the show on which Sinéad would sing two songs, a not-so-nice Brooklyn boy named Andrew Silverstein who performed under the name Andrew "Dice" Clay. In his "Dice-man" character, Silverstein either—depending on one's point of view—speared liberal sacred cows or advocated the most vicious kind of hatefulness. Clay's material (not jokes so much as incessant put-downs) was homophobic, sexist, racist, size-ist, xenophobic, and, perhaps most important, not funny. Many people who despise Sam Kinison's material, for example, tolerate it a bit because the man is capable of occasional jaw-dropping hilarity: he is a guilty pleasure. Clay, who has the misfortune of not being able to marry his hate to a single funny joke, is far less interesting. His act consists of nursery rhymes turned into grade-school-bathroom one-liners ("Little boy blew. He needed the money") and unformed attacks on groups who cannot fight back, like new immigrants who work the overnight shifts at convenience stores, and AIDS victims. But the predominant aspect of his "act" is his hatred (probably a manifestation of fear) of women. He finds no use for women who are not on their knees before him, and even that leaves him unsatisfied. He uses expletive-laden anger to cloak his own fear of inadequacy; he is the comic equivalent of the bully who kicks and runs.

The week before the "Saturday Night Live" episode, someone alerted Sinéad to what Clay was all about, and she was appalled. She pondered what she should do about it, but "Saturday Night Live" regular cast member Nora Dunn made it easier for her. On the Tuesday before the show with Clay as host, Dunn decided she had to boycott it. Calling Clay's act "hateful," she told the Associated Press: "I love 'Saturday Night Live' and I feel loyal to my colleagues, my cast members, and the writers of the show, and I respect them very much, but I will not perform with Andrew Dice Clay and I don't want to be associated with him and I oppose his work. I don't want to be part of providing an arena for him to make himself legitimate because I don't think he is. Although I feel he has a right to express himself, I have a right to strongly state my position." She went on to argue that popularity is not sufficient for someone to get a booking: "If I was booking the show in the thirties, I wouldn't book Adolf Hitler simply because he's chancellor and has a big following."

That hyperbole is not as effective as, say, Sinéad's in "Black Boys on Mopeds," but this is not supposed to be art. It did make clear how reprehensible Dunn finds Clay's work. The other female cast members of "Saturday Night Live" kept mum on the subject, including Victoria Jackson, who had appeared with Clay in a notably untitillating movie called **Casual Sex?** Dunn is not a great performer by any stretch of the imagination, but she clearly thought about what she was going to say about Clay before she opened her mouth. She was not trying to censor Clay, as some have; all she said was that she did not want to be part of anything involving him.

Dunn's reasoning and Sinéad's conscience left Sinéad with only one course of action. The next day, publicist Schock released a statement that read, in part: "It would be nonsensical of 'Saturday Night Life' to expect a woman to perform songs about a woman's experiences after a monologue by Andrew Dice Clay." Skeptics argued that Sinéad had a number one album and single and did not need the exposure, but one cannot damn someone for having the leverage to act on her conscience. The two acts who replaced her, David Lynch chanteuse Julee Cruise and father-son rockabilly team the Spanic Boys, were grateful for the break and did not think twice about the last-minute offer. But the speculation that surrounded her refusal to perform was foolish and lazily whimsical. Maybe if Sinéad was on the dole and fifty thousand pounds in debt, she might have gone on the show. This is like one of those ridiculous hypothetical questions some reporters ask politicians; the scenario is so farfetched that it is not worth dignifying with an analysis. Worse, such a suggestion implies that Sinéad's whole career has been a fake, which is so cynical that it is not worth dignifying with a retort. One can argue with Sinéad's behavior if one wants, but one cannot satisfactorily argue that she has ever put financial considerations before artistic ones. Doing so would be wrongheaded and petty.

It would not, however, be as wrongheaded or petty as "Saturday Night Live" executive producer Lorne Michaels's cynical decision to retain Clay for the show and let Sinéad and Dunn go. He showed no loyalty to Dunn, a staff member who should have been more important to him than Clay, someone who would breeze in for a week, smell up the place, and skedaddle. As Boston Celtics guru Red Auerbach has said, "Loyalty is a two-way street." If a boss shows no loyalty to his subordinates, he will receive none in return. And he let Sinéad slip away during a week when she held the number one spots on **Billboard**'s single and album charts. Michaels is no fool—he knew that Clay was a media freak who will be reduced to a Trivial Pursuit stumper in a few months—and he wanted to get Clay on his show during the few weeks that people knew who he was.

At the time, Michaels let loose with empty rhetoric about how giving Clay a forum to disseminate hate some-how was a great victory for believers in the First Amendment. What he did not bother to say at the time was that within hours after Sinéad pulled out of the show, "Saturday Night Live" talent coordinator Liz Welch received a phone call from representatives of the incendiary rap group Public Enemy, offering to appear on the show, then only four days away. They were rejected out of hand.

If there was any censorship involved in that "Saturday Night Live" episode, it was when the show turned down Public Enemy. The group was just as controversial as Clay (perhaps more so, because they were African-Americans with a grudge against the white power structure) and they had an enormous following; their platinum **Fear of a Black Planet** album was the second-fastest-selling record in the country, behind **I Do Not Want What I Haven't Got**.

But "Saturday Night Live" officials figured they had enough controversy for the night with Clay, and for musical guests they felt it would be safe to go with relatively unknown, certainly more mannered performers like Cruise and the Spanics. "Saturday Night Live" always boasts that it is on the cutting edge of television, but their decision to reject Public Enemy was cowardly and possibly racist. It was the sort of television programming decision Michaels frequently derides.

Michaels could have been a hero if he'd wanted to be. He could have forged some much-needed solidarity in the ranks of the "Saturday Night Live" staff, which had been one large dysfunctional family from the start. He could have rallied behind a performer who had a conscience as well as an audience in the millions. He should have dumped Clay, but he wanted a quick fix. There should have been nothing controversial about Dunn's and Sinéad's decisions to stay away from Clay; they were class moves, but Michaels's selfish intransigence and need for publicity revved up a hurricane of interest.

Michaels got his way, and the May 12 episode of "Saturday Night Live" was the highest-rated installment of the season, which is no big deal considering the erosion of the show's audience. But Dunn and Sinéad had the best revenge: the show was even more horrible than usual that night.

The opening sketch was a takeoff on the Frank Capra fantasy **It's a Wonderful Life**, in which Clay felt horrible about his life and contemplated suicide. (No doubt some viewers were cheering him on.) Instead of the Angel Clarence, who guided star Jimmy Stewart in the film, the Devil, played by Jon Lovitz, shows up and tells Clay to stop his whining. The Devil then takes Clay on a tour to show him how the world would have been different without him. At once it is evident that Clay has no more acting talent than Brooke Shields or Tor Johnson: he reads cue cards and hopes he puts the emphasis on the right words.

The Devil tells Clay that, had he not agreed to host "Saturday Night Live" that night, Frank Zappa would have hosted the show and delivered a seventy-minute rant against censorship. One of Sinéad's amplifiers would have fallen on Dunn's head, killing her. Sinéad would be so devastated she would lose the will to sing.

"That's too bad," Clay non-emoted. "She was a cute, bald chick."

Later in the show, cast member Jan Hooks did a short piece in which she announced, "I didn't boycott because, frankly, I didn't have the guts." It was unclear whether it was a joke; it certainly was not funny. The cast members were trying to turn the boycott into something, but because it was clear they did not understand what was at stake, their words fell far short.

A few months later, Sinéad was still on a sold-out tour, Dunn had appeared in the critically acclaimed film **Miami Blues**, and "Saturday Night Live" still faded away each episode after the first two sketches. As for Clay, he had already begun his inevitable fade into oblivion. The first film in which he starred, **The Adventures of Ford Fairlane**, bombed, his much-hyped in-concert film was shelved, and he got kicked off Geffen Records. Eventually he will get an unimportant seat on "Hollywood Squares" or something and turn into Charles Nelson Reilly.

Nine days after she was supposed to perform on "Saturday Night Live," Sinéad showed up at a soundstage on the South Side of old Chicago to appear in a video for "The Emperor's New Clothes." It was a strong choice for a second single off **I Do Not Want What I Haven't Got**, and it was one of the sturdiest parts of the live show. But if the video for "Nothing Compares 2 U" was that rare song commercial that deepened one's appreciation of the song, even fans who loved "The Emperor's New Clothes" had to admit that the best way to enjoy the song was to avoid the video. It was a solo lip-synch, not a live performance, that featured Sinéad on a small vaudeville stage dressed in a black gown trying to look funky while a diverse audience either paid attention to her or knitted. There was no energy in the video, not a point to it. The song remained sparkling, but the muddiness of the video helped ensure that "The Emperor's New Clothes" would not be a major hit single.

The tour carried on, Sinéad jettisoned Hugh Harris (he was dropped from the tour when he was dropped from her life), and she became involved with several all-star projects. Through the summer, she dedicated "The Last Day of Our Acquaintance" to either "all the women here tonight" or Andrew Dice Clay. Sinéad committed to an October show in Chile benefiting Amnesty International, in which she would share the stage with the usual rock-conscience folk (Sting, Peter Gabriel, Jackson Browne) as well as those temporary icons of the training-bra set, New Kids on the Block.

Another project to which Sinéad contributed was **Red, Hot, and Blue: A Benefit for AIDS Research and Relief**. It was a series of short films of performers singing Cole Porter songs, an interesting concept since Porter wrote articulately and wryly about love and sex while at the same time he had had to hide his homosexuality to be able to keep working. Sinéad contributed a version of "You Do Something to Me," with a film shot by John Maybury in which she wore a period wig that evoked both Veronika Lake and Jayne Mansfield. She also performed the song, backed by a twenty-three-piece orchestra, at a June press conference announcing the project. Some of the more noteworthy other musicians involved with the project were David Byrne, Neneh Cherry, Fine Young

Cannibals, k. d. lang, the Neville Brothers, and Sinéad's pals in U2; the list of other filmmakers included Percy Adlon, Pedro Almodóvar, Jonathan Demme, and Wim Wenders.

Sinéad's most bombastic extracurricular musical activity took place on July 21 in Berlin, when she was part of Roger Waters's **The Wall** extravaganza. Nothing much came from the event, except that Sinéad sang an undermiked "Mother," she played with former members of the Band Rick Danko, Levon Helm, and Garth Hudson, and she got her picture taken with her idol Van Morrison. Two hundred thousand people attended the concert; virtually none of them heard her sing.

Press attention toward Sinéad increased around this time. After someone broke the Harris story (or the Harris affair—it was not a news story) and Sinéad postponed two shows in the Midwest in early August, some genius decided that the two factoids added up to inarguable evidence that Sinéad was pregnant and suffering from, as one tabloid put it, "severe morning sickness." It was all sensational nonsense, and probably the only solace Sinéad could draw from the media-circus atmosphere that enveloped her was that it could never get any worse than this. This would pass, and then she would be allowed to have her life back.

She was wrong.

On August 24, Sinéad and her band pulled off the Garden State Parkway in Holmdel, New Jersey, to play at the Garden State Arts Center. It was a typical day of show: soundcheck and wait.

Shortly before she was to go onstage, Sinéad learned that the custom at the Arts Center was to play "The Star-Spangled Banner," the national anthem of the United States, before each show. Sinéad was puzzled; then she was livid. It made no sense to her and she demanded that the anthem not be played. Arts Center officials told her she had no choice, but the truth was that *they* had no choice: there were nine thousand people waiting to hear Sinéad. The New Jersey Highway Authority, which runs the Arts Center, allowed her to go on so as to avoid trouble, but informed Sinéad that she was banned from the Arts Center for life.

The Highway Authority got first dibs in this affair on self-righteous acts that backfired. They got the yahoo vote by banning Sinéad, but with the touring market as soft as it was in 1990 (and was likely to be in 1991), they were foolish to deny themselves one of the few non-dinosaur acts who can guarantee a sellout. With most Arts Center concerts barely breaking even, they had no right—and no leverage—to complain.

The second idiot on board was Frank Sinatra, who played the Arts Center the next night. **USA Today** quoted Sinatra's onstage remarks about Sinéad as, "She should not have been permitted to go on. If she didn't like it, she should have just left." In fact, Ol' Blue Eyes spoke in terms far less gracious or coherent. He really said, "This Sinéad O'Connor, this must be one stupid broad. I understand she said some things. I'm not even going to repeat them. I'd kick her ass if she were a guy. She must beat her kids to stay in shape." Typical comments from a man with a history of allegedly brutalizing women, to be sure, but this was reaching, even for him.

Sinéad treated Sinatra's outburst as dismissively as was appropriate, telling **MTV News** that Sinatra needed the press, and suggested to **Entertainment Today** that "it's probably very important to Frank that he thinks the American authorities are on his side." A few weeks later the cranky Sinatra moved on to getting mad at George

Michael for having second thoughts about wiggling his butt for MTV cameras.

Still, Sinéad realized that she had to address the issue. The day after the Sinatra concert, she told **USA Today** that she did not see what anthems had to do with her, her music, or her fans. She said she did not mean to be disrespectful, and that she disapproved of playing after any anthem, not just that of the United States. Nonetheless, she had strong feelings about going on after "The Star-Spangled Banner." She said, "I feel very strongly about censorship, and I don't want to go onstage after the anthem of a country that's arresting people and harassing people for expressing themselves onstage." She added, "I sincerely harbor no disrespect for America or Americans." She referred to censored artists as "her friends" and encouraged solidarity with them.

From a media point of view, Sinéad's mistake was issuing an intelligent statement and implicitly championing the oft-arrested rap group 2 Live Crew at a time when censorship wars were raging hard, over everything from NC-17–rated movies and rap music to Robert Mapplethorpe's photographs. Also, Sinéad's well-reasoned anthem veto came barely a month after sitcom star Roseanne Barr made fun of the anthem while "singing" it before a San Diego Padres baseball game. Barr was joking, Sinéad was smart and serious, but that did not stop many from likening their two acts. Rather than deal with the underlying issues that are dragging down the United States, American politicians encouraged their constituents to be as empty-minded as they and argue about symbols. The legality of burning the American flag was a key issue in the vapid 1988 presidential election; protecting the war-glorifying "The Star-Spangled Banner" was on the same low level. Why talk about censorship and racism when you can argue about trivia? Within forty-eight hours of Sinéad's Arts Center show, New York state senator Nicholas Spano called for a boycott, and helped organize a protest in Saratoga, which Sinéad attended incognito in a brown wig and baseball cap. Spano must have had something better to do. Nearly everyone else did: only a dozen other people showed up.

The third blockhead on the bandwagon was the **New York Post**, which ran blanket coverage that encouraged other newspapers to treat the story as if it were news. The cover of the August 27 **Post** showed a picture of Sinéad at the Grammy Awards with the page-filling headline "IRISH SINGER SNUBS U.S." For balance there was a microscopic reference to the Persian Gulf crisis at the bottom of the page. The coverage inside was even more off-kilter. The three inside stories about Sinéad (three more stories than the paper ran that day about homelessness) were by Cathy Burke, whose grasp of the issues involved seemed formed by Sinatra's phalanx of publicists and apologists. She compared Sinéad to Barr in her lead sentence, and only quoted sources from the Highway Authority, which had embarked on nothing less than a smear campaign. Burke wrote that "a call to her publicist, Elaine Schock, went unreturned yesterday." Of course it remained unreturned: who sits in their office on a Sunday in August? A sidebar is even more hilarious: Burke refers to the rarely published Legs McNeil as a "noted rock journalist," and misuses the word "politics" at every turn. No wonder the **Post** had Burke working on a summer Sunday.

The fourth wheel on this self-righteous road to nowhere was contributed by radio disk jockeys, who made Cathy Burke's **Post** pieces seem like Pulitzer-worthy material. The program director for New York's WHTZ-FM (Z100) displayed a disk jockey's typical lack of comprehension of complex issues when he said, "No anthem. No hair. No more hits on Z100. Let her have a nice career in some other country." When Boston disk jockey Scott McKenzie was asked why he was banning Sinéad's music, he said, "It was the obvious thing to do, especially right now, with the Mideast thing. We just don't need this." Archie Bunker lives.

Schock, finally reached for comment (**Billboard** waited until Monday to call), had the last word: "These stations are doing it for publicity purposes. I don't believe that any of their protests are heartfelt." She also pointed out that none of the stations in question ever addressed the issue of why Sinéad did what she did.

For her part, Sinéad just tried to keep the tour moving, with one change: she added the Bob Marley and the Wailers song about demanding freedom, "Get Up, Stand Up," to her set. Sinéad was not exactly born to play reggae, but the Marley cover was a calm, thought-out gesture, which means it had nothing in common with the simpleminded attacks on her.

A week later, Sinéad found herself at the Universal Amphitheater, in Universal City, California, attending the MTV Video Awards, which in its seven years of existence had become just as glitzy and contrived as the Grammy Awards and the American Music Awards. Sinéad was nominated for four awards, including Best Video of the Year. The show has gone brain-dead Hollywood, as evidenced by its inevitable host, Arsenio Hall. As director Oliver Stone said before presenting an award, "Video has given me a whole new way to look at visuals." Oh.

As at the Grammys two years earlier, it was clear that the establishment still did not "get" Sinéad. In an interview just before the show started, Billy Idol—a labelmate, for Pete's sake, whose promotional budget was probably funded by Sinéad proceeds—suggested that Sinéad would win the award for Best Male Video. It figured that Andrew Dice Clay had picked Idol to write songs for his failed movie.

That night Sinéad performed her nominated number "Nothing Compares 2 U," complete with extended coda, in a translucent white gown, and she was one of the few performers who genuinely performed live (although after hearing Motley Crue play live, one could be forgiven for wishing that they had lip-synched). Although Sinéad had monitor problems, she delivered a version of her hit that built on her recorded version and moved on. She won three of the four awards for which she had been nominated—Best Female Video, Best Post-Modern Video (whatever that means), and Best Video of the Year. She seemed genuinely surprised to be stealing the show, and she and director Maybury looked like giddy kids. When she won the prime award, she thanked Prince, her managers past and present, her husband (gossip writers harrumphed), her band, and "Mr. God" (four winning performers had thanked God; by the end of the evening it had become a running joke).

Then she got serious. "I have a great respect for people of all countries, including the American people. My attitude over the national anthem was in order to draw attention to the censorship issue. When it's racism disguised as censorship, it's even worse, and that's the point I was trying to make."

The auditorium erupted even louder than they had when she sang earlier in the evening. Sinéad was being honored as a visual icon, but at her moment of greatest industry acclamation, she insisted on bringing substance to the moment. She insisted that ideas held sway over image. For that moment, she was at the top of the world, and she had brought an industry up there with her.

EPILOGUE

The Blue Bird Flies

*O*n September 29, 1990, after everyone involved had calmed down, Sinéad showed up on the sixteenth season premiere of "Saturday Night Live." It was a gracious gesture, but things had changed. Nora Dunn was gone from the cast, and even though the show's writing staff had a long summer to think up new jokes, the night's skits were as vacuous as the ones they usually toss together in six days.

Sinéad performed two songs that night from behind purple-tinted John Lennon spectacles, and she came on with more straightforward rock-and-roll attitude than usual. "Three Babies," the first tune, was a warmup. Her voice sounded as strained as a rock voice sounds toward the end of a long tour and when she paced in circles during the synthesizer break it seemed that she was walking to keep herself interested. Far superior, after the admonition "I'd like to dedicate this song to women everywhere," was "The Last Day of Our Acquaintance." Its solo acoustic beginning hushed the studio audience, but the song got stronger, deeper, and finally crashed into full-blown rock and roll, drums and guitars screaming into the night. Sinéad played the song like the punk that the press, especially in England, always wanted her to be. She danced, spun around, shouted; she was a great rock star, professional, hearty, living up to her reputation. She was finally on "Saturday Night Live," on her own terms.

As her 1990 tour wound down and Sinéad counted down the hours to when she could hibernate from the media, the few interviews she granted concentrated on how unhappy she was with her superstardom. She wanted her life back, she said, and she would do what she had to to reclaim it. To her, "fame" had become an obscenity.

Yet Sinéad was trying to have it both ways. If she is going to boast about how her audience loves her because her work is so personal and autobiographical, and then spin around and say that her life is none of her audience's business, she is clearly confused. If she hates being a star, she should stop doing videos, stop putting her picture on the cover of her records, stop doing interviews. Publicity is a necessary, albeit occasionally distasteful, side effect of stardom. Like most thinking rock stars, Sinéad appreciates the adulation but wishes she had a faucet that could control it. Still, her "honest" comments on the ravages of fame sometimes sounded petulant. It had been a long year. (Her comments at the time about how racism by rappers was not nearly as reprehensible as that by white people also smacked of exhaustion.)

Nineteen ninety was Sinéad's most triumphant and most painful year. She became an irreversible superstar; at the same time she had terrible trouble maintaining relationships with those closest to her. What is most lasting about **I Do Not Want What I Haven't Got** is how Sinéad transformed a wide variety of experiences, painful and transcendent, into a cycle of tremendous songs. The year 1990 was a wild one for her, with experiences diverse and intense enough to suggest that the next Sinéad record will be something worth waiting for.

Sinéad O'Connor Discography (1983–1990)

With In Tua Nua
"Take My Hand" (Island single, 1983, out of print)

With the Edge
Soundtrack to **The Captive** (Virgin, 1986)
Sinéad sings one cut: "Heroine" (theme from **The Captive**); (music by the Edge; lyrics by the Edge and Sinéad O'Connor).

With World Party (Kurt Wallinger's group)
Private Revolution (Chrysalis/Ensign, 1986)
Sinéad sings backing vocals on one cut. She also appears in the video for "Private Revolution."

With World Party
Goodbye Jumbo (Chrysalis/Ensign, 1990)
Sinéad sings backing vocals on one cut: "Sweet Soul Dream."

The Albums

The Lion and the Cobra (Chrysalis/Ensign, 1987)
Produced by Sinéad O'Connor; coproduced and engineered by Kevin Moloney; mixed by Sinéad O'Connor, Kevin Moloney, and Fachtna O'Ceallaigh. Tracks: Jackie/Mandinka/Jerusalem/Just Like U Said It Would B/Never Get Old/Troy/I Want Your (Hands on Me)/Drink Before the War/Just Call Me Joe.

I Do Not Want What I Haven't Got (Chrysalis/Ensign, 1990)
Produced by Sinéad O'Connor, except "Nothing Compares 2 U" produced by Sinéad O'Connor and Nellee Hooper; engineered by Chris Birkett, except "Three Babies" engineered by Chris Birkett and Sean Devitt. Tracks: Feel So Different/I Am Stretched on Your Grave/Three Babies/The Emperor's New Clothes/Black Boys on Mopeds/Nothing Compares 2 U/Jump in the River/You Cause As Much Sorrow/The Last Day of Our Acquaintance/I Do Not Want What I Haven't Got.

Selected B-sides and Oddities

Live at the Paradise (bootleg, 1988)
This is a portion of a live broadcast on WBCN-FM of O'Connor's first Boston appearance, at the Paradise Rock Club. Songs include: Jackie/Mandinka/Never Get Old/Just Like U Said It Would B/Jerusalem/Smith's Song/Just Call Me Joe/I Want Your (Hands on Me).

I Want Your (Hands on Me) (Chrysalis/Ensign, 1988)
M. C. Lyte produced by Audio Two; "Just Call Me Joe"
produced by Paul Watts
This four-cut twelve-inch single includes three new mixes
of the track from **The Lion and the Cobra**, augmented by
rapper M. C. Lyte. The fourth track is a live version of
"Just Call Me Joe," recorded at BBC Radio One.

Jump in the River (Chrysalis/Ensign, 1988)
Karen Finley produced by Mark Kamins
This three-cut, twelve-inch single includes two versions of
the title track, one an extended mix augmented by provocative performance artist Karen Finley, and **The Lion and
the Cobra** version of "Jerusalem."

The Wall (PolyGram, 1990)
Accompanied by members of the Band, O'Connor sang
"Mother" at Roger Waters's over-the-top Berlin produc-
tion of the Pink Floyd rock opera.

The Emperor's New Clothes, (Chrysalis/Ensign, 1990)
"The Emperor's New Clothes," remixed by Hank Shocklee,
EOS, and Gary G-Wiz; "Mandinka" remixed by Paul
"Groucho" Smykle. This four-cut CD single includes two
versions of the title cut, including a remixed version for
dance clubs with a completely new rhythm track. Also
included are "What Do You Want?" (an outtake from
the Mick Glossop sessions that also appears on the
flip-side of the two-track cassette single) and a new
sound-effects-laden version of "Mandinka," labeled "Jake's
Remix."

The Emperor's New Clothes (Chrysalis/Ensign, 1990)

"The Emperor's New Clothes" remixed by Hank Shocklee, EOS, and Gary G-Wiz; "I Am Stretched on Your Grave" remixed by Bill Coleman with Super D.J. Dmitry and Jungle D.J. Towa Towa. The twelve-inch vinyl single is considerably different from its CD-single counterpart. The first side contains two versions of the title tune, both the remixed version from the CD single and an edited version of the same. The second side offers two remixes of "I Am Stretched on Your Grave," again intended for dance-club use. Incidentally, the seven-inch single of "The Emperor's New Clothes" is shorter than the album version, omitting most of the extended instrumental coda.

Red, Hot, and Blue: A Benefit for AIDS Research and Relief (Chrysalis, 1990)

For this benefit record of Cole Porter tunes, Sinéad recorded a version of "You Do Something to Me." At a June 1990 press conference announcing the project, she performed the tune accompanied by a twenty-three-piece orchestra.

Selected Videography
(1987–1990)

Official Videos

Troy (1987, 10min 16sec)
Director: John Maybury
Includes much of "Never Get Old" and snatches of other tracks from **The Lion and the Cobra**.

Jump in the River (1988, 4min 10sec)
Director: John Maybury

I Want Your (Hands on Me) (1988, 4min 52sec)
Director: John Maybury
M. C. Lyte appears in this video.

Mandinka (1988, 3min 44sec)
Director: John Maybury

Nothing Compares 2 U (1989, 5min 6sec)
Director: John Maybury
Winner, three MTV awards.

The Value of Ignorance (1989, 35min 12sec)
Director: John Maybury
Recorded live at London's Dominion Theater, June 1988;
Songs: Jackie/Just Like U Said It Would B/Mandinka/Just
Call Me Joe/Never Get Old/Jerusalem/Troy/I Am Stretched
on Your Grave [a cappella version].

The Emperor's New Clothes (1990, 4min 26sec)
Director: Sophie Milken

Three Babies (1990, 4min 47sec)
Director: John Maybury

You Do Something to Me (1990, 2min 34sec)
Director: John Maybury

Selected U.S. Television Appearances

Grammy Awards, February 1989
Lip-synchs to "Mandinka."

"On the Edge" with Maria Shriver, August 1990
Relatively revealing interview in spite of Shriver's surface-
level questions; good, brief performance footage.

MTV Awards, September 1990
Pre-show interview with Kurt Loder; strong live performance of "Nothing Compares 2 U"; wins three of the four
awards for which she was nominated.

ACKNOWLEDGMENTS

*M*any people helped, but blame me for whatever went wrong.

Thanks to Amanda Joy Rubin for yeoman photo research and Cindy Redmond at Chrysalis Records in New York for prompt responses to unreasonable requests. Thanks also to Elaine Schock for not putting up any roadblocks, to Oedipus for the ticket and the tapes, to Noel E. Monk for not taking anything personally, and to T.P. for the last minute.

For their encouragement and support, thanks to the usual crew of affable misfits: Mark Caro and the Mark Caro Shufflin' Crew, John "Soul Brother Number One" Guterman, expert closet designer Janestein and Sister, King of Nashville Andrew McLenon, world boxball champion Owen O'Donnell, ace debater Tim Riley, and, of course, George L. Tirebiter. Thanks also to Anatole Broyard for teaching me how to "go on."

On the side, thanks to Kerry Rodensky Timbers at Bromberg and Sunstein.

Personal thanks to the Scheys and the Kokernaks.

Most of all, thanks to Charlie Conrad at Warner Books. Conrad is an ideal, "artless" editor; every writer should be lucky enough to work with someone as committed and encouraging.

ABOUT THE AUTHOR

JIMMY GUTERMAN is the author of *12 Days on the Road* and several other books. He has written for a wide variety of publications, among them *Spy, Rolling Stone*, the *Village Voice*, and the *Boston Phoenix*.